TURNING DEBTS INTO DOLLARS

ABOUT THE AUTHOR

Dan A. Wolner is National Credit Manager for Harmon Glass Company, Minneapolis, MN, and has 20 years credit and collection management experience. He graduated from the University of Minnesota in 1970, and received his CCE award in 1990. In 1992, Wolner was elected to a three-year term on the NACM North Central Board of Directors. Dan is past chair of the Transportation Industry Credit Group.

In addition to the NACM bookshelf title, "Turning Debts into Dollars," Wolner is the co-author of the NACM publication, "Principles of Business Collections." He serves on the Editorial Advisory Council of NACM's monthly magazine, "Business Credit," and is a regular contributing author to the magazine. Dan has been the featured speaker at local and regional NACM meetings. Wolner received the NACM North Central's 1993 Credit Executive of the Year award.

TURNING DEBTS INTO DOLLARS:
A Common Sense Guide to Extending Credit & Collecting Money

Dan A. Wolner, CCE

Dan A. Wolner, Publisher
Minneapolis, Minnesota

Dan A. Wolner, Publisher

This publication is designed to provide accurate, current information with regard to the subject matter covered. It is intended to help people engaged in business maintain and expand their competence. This publication is sold with the understanding that Dan A. Wolner is not engaged in rendering legal, accounting, or other professional advice. If legal advice or expert assistance is required, the service of a competent professional should be sought. Those using this publication in dealing with specific legal, accounting or other business matters should research original sources of authority.

ISBN 0-86678-428-4

Copyright © 1986, 1989, 1994 by Dan A. Wolner, Publisher

All rights reserved. No part of this publication may be reproduced or transmitted in any form or by any means, electronic or mechanical, including photocopy, recording, or any information retrieval system, without permission in writing from the publisher:

Dan A. Wolner, Publisher
P.O. Box 39657, Minneapolis, MN 55439-0657

Printed in the United States of America

First Edition 1986
Second Edition 1989
Third Edition 1994

*Dedicated to my loving wife, Teresa
and my daughter, Elizabeth.*

Contents

Preface xv

Acknowledgments xvii

Introduction xix

PART I. CREDIT – GRANTING STRATEGY   1

1 **Factors Affecting Your Strategy**   3

   Reasons for Extending Credit   3
   Company Credit and Sales Philosophy   4
   Company Resources   5
   Past Success in Controlling Receivables   6
   Other Elements   7

2 **Selecting a Strategy**   13

3 **Getting to Know Prospective Customers**   15

   Credit Applications   15
      Consumer Credit Applications   19
      Commercial Credit Applications   21
      Other Considerations   22
   Trade References   23
      Verifying Trade Credit Information   23
      Right to Trade Credit Information   24

Form of Request   25
Rights of Inquiry   25
Other Considerations   27
Bank References   28
General Rules   29
Civic, Credit, and Trade Associations   32

4 **Additional Sources of Information**   35

Personal Interviews   35
Credit-Reporting Services   36
Financial Statements   39

5 **Making a Credit-Granting Decision**   45

Who Makes the Decision?   45
Information Needed to Make a Decision   47
Saying "No"   48
Softening the Blow   49

6 **Setting Credit Limits**   51

New Customers   51
Established Customers   52

7 **Making the Strategy Work**   55

Information Management   55
An Untapped Source of Credit Information   55
Motivation   56
Training   56
Communication   57

PART II. COLLECTING ACCOUNTS ACCORDING TO APPROVED TERMS   59

8 **Why People Don't Pay on Time**   61

9 **Collection Follow-Up** 65
   Spotting Potential Problems 65
   Developing a Follow-Up System 66
   Timing 66
   Easing into the Collection Process 67
   Handling Responses to Initial Inquiries 69

10 **The Impact of Past-Due Receivables** 71

11 **Writing Effective Collection Letters** 79
   Eight Cardinal Rules 79
   Five Essential Elements of a Collection Letter 82
       The Identifier 82
       The Grabber 83
       The Clarifier 84
       The Motivator 85
       The Concluder 85
   Practical Applications 87
       Analysis of the "Before" and "After" Collection Letters 98
   Staying Out of Trouble 99

12 **Telephone Collection Strategies** 101
   The Five Phases of a Collection Call 102
       Precall Preparation 102
       Identification of the Parties 105
       Fact-Finding 106
       Reaching an Agreement 111
       Following Up 116
       Faxing 117

PART III. ALTERNATIVE COLLECTION MEASURES 119

Why Alternative Collection Measures Are Needed 119
When to Use Alternative Collection Measures 119
The Options 120
Choosing an Alternative Collection Measure 121

13 Settlements   123

　Arriving at a Settlement Offer   123
　Structure   124
　Timing   124
　A Practical Example   124
　Deciding Whether to Settle   125
　Two Final Points   125

14 Small Claims Court   127

　Filing Requirements   127
　Deciding Whether to Use Small Claims Court   128
　Filing Suit   129
　Notification of the Parties   130
　Counterclaims   130
　Appearing in Court   133
　Failing to Appear   133
　Notification of a Decision   133
　Collecting a Judgment   134
　Executing a Judgment   136
　When Assets Cannot Be Located   140
　Should You Use Small Claims Court?   140

15 Collection Agencies   145

　When to Use a Collection Agency   145
　Selecting the Right Type   146
　Before Making a Selection   147
　Protecting Yourself from Unscrupulous Agencies   150
　The Cost   152
　Guidelines for Collection Agency Users   154

16 Collection Attorneys   157

　The Collection Attorney's Role   158
　The Cost   159
　Dissatisfaction with the Attorney   159
　Additional Points   160

17 **Alternative Dispute Resolution** 163
   What is Mediation? 163
   When Mediation Should Be Used 164
   Structuring the Mediation Process 164
   Collecting Money 166
   Finding a Competent Mediator 167
   Arbitration 167
   NACM ADR Program 168
   Hearings 168

Conclusion 171

Appendix

A. Readability Index 173

B. Equal Credit Opportunity Act 175
   Creditworthiness 175
   Equal Credit Opportunity 175
   Questions About an Applicant's Sex, Marital Status, or Age 176
   Rating Credit Applicants as a Credit Risk 176
   Extending Credit—Opening and Maintaining Individual Accounts 178
   Establishing a Credit History 179
   Notice and Penalties 180
   The Most Important Rules 180

C. Fair Credit Reporting Act 183
   When Reports May Be Issued 183
   When Credit is Denied on the Basis of a Credit Report 183
   When Credit Bureau Reports Contribute to Credit Denials 184
   Limitations on Adverse Information 184
   Special Investigations 184
   What Type of Information Should a Credit Granter Disclose? 185
   Government Agencies 185

D. Fair Credit Billing Act   187

   Billing Errors   187
   In Case of Error   187
   Credit Ratings   188
   Defective Merchandise or Services   189
   Penalties and Other Provisions   189

E. Skiptracing Guide   191

   Traits of a Good Skiptracer   191
   Getting the Information You Need   192
   Skiptracing Resources   193

F. Fair Debt Collection Practices Act   195

   The Scope of the Law   195
   Locating a Customer   195
   Contacting the Customer   196
   Prohibited Tactics   196
   Validating the Debt   197
   Legal Remedies   197

G. State Collection Agency Licensing Authorities   199

Figures

1. Calculating Dollar Days Outstanding   8
2. Commercial Credit Applications   16, 17
3. Consumer Credit Application   18
4. Letter Requesting Bank Information   31
5. Letter Presenting Check to Bank as Collection Item   33
6. Credit Report   37
7. Balance Sheet   41
8. Ratio Calculations   42
9. Reminder Letter   68
10 – 14. "Before" and "After" Collection Letters   88
15. Small Claims Court Claim Form   131
16. Satisfaction of Judgment   135

17A. Affidavit of Identification of Judgment Debtor   137
17B. Writ of Execution   138
17C. Request for Order for Disclosure   139
18. Garnishment Exemption Notice   141
19. Balance Confirmation Letter   153

Graphs

1. Ratio of Aftertax Corporate Domestic Profits to Corporate Domestic Income   72
2. Bank Rates on Short-Term Business Loans   73

Tables

1. Additional Sales Dollars Needed to Overcome a Given Bad-Debt Loss at a Given Profit Margin   74
2. Net Profit in Dollars on a Given Sale at a Given Profit Margin   74
3. Small Claims Court Jurisdictional Limits   143

Index   203

PREFACE

This book was written to answer the question: "How can I use my common sense and knowledge of people to grant credit and collect money confidently, economically, effectively, ethically, and legally?" Although the book doesn't contain a magic formula that will solve all credit and collection problems, it will help you avoid such problems by teaching you to think. You'll learn the ins and outs of receivables control and benefit from years of experience and knowledge. My background as a credit manager, collection agency manager, sales manager, corporate officer, small business owner, consultant, educator, and public speaker will give you a unique insight into credit management.

If you have comments, questions, suggestions, or criticisms when you have finished reading this book, please write to me:

> Dan A. Wolner, Publisher
> P.O. Box 39657
> Minneapolis, MN 55439-0657

ACKNOWLEDGEMENTS

I am most grateful to:

The Reverend Robert H. Schuller, for teaching me the importance of "possibility thinking."

The following organizations, for their contributions and assistance: Board of Governors, Federal Reserve System; U.S. Commerce Department, Bureau of Economic Analysis; Minneapolis Mediation Center; Minnesota Lawyers' Professional Responsibility Board; National Association of Credit Management (NACM).

All my past and present business associates, co-workers, clients, and supporters across the country, for sharing their ideas and experiences with me.

My parents, Harlan and Eva Lou Wolner, for a lifetime of support and devotion.

INTRODUCTION

Congratulations! You've just made one of the wisest decisions you'll ever be asked to make. You've decided to do something about one of the thorniest problems confronting people in business.

This book is a straightforward, easy to understand guide to credit and collections divided into three parts. Part I, "Basic Credit Granting," will start you down the path toward more confident credit granting. Part II, "Collecting Accounts According to Approved Terms," will provide you with the information you need to collect your money. Part III, "Alternative Collection Measures," proposes alternatives designed to help you deal with customers who don't respond to your usual collection methods.

More specifically, Part I will help you choose a workable credit-granting strategy by exploring factors such as your credit policy, the financial health of your company and the companies you serve, your past success in controlling receivables, and other elements. You'll discover how important it is to learn all you can about your customers by gathering credit information from a variety of sources, including credit applications; trade references; bank references; civic, credit, and trade associations; personal interviews with credit applicants; credit-reporting services; financial statements; and even your own company personnel. And you'll learn the importance of verifying the information you gather. The differences between consumer and commercial credit transactions are discussed, including the legal ramifications of granting or not granting credit. You'll learn what you must and must not say when denying credit to someone, and you'll receive assistance in setting credit limits for both new and existing customers.

Part II will help you react appropriately to slow-pay and no-pay accounts. It will help you understand why people pay late and show you how to handle reluctant, hostile, even abusive customers. You'll learn to identify the signs that usually foreshadow collection problems. You'll discover why it's so crucial to get all the facts before you "lower the boom" on delinquent customers. You'll learn the importance of resolving little problems before they escalate into big problems. Specific guidelines are given to direct your collection efforts, whether you're collecting by letter or telephone. You'll learn the value of persistence, and you'll be shown the importance of focusing your attention on potential solutions to problems, not on the problems themselves.

Part III will help you decide what to do when nothing else seems to work. It discusses a wide range of collection alternatives, including settlements, small claims court, collection agencies, collection attorneys, and alternative dispute resolution(ADR). You'll learn when it's best to swallow your pride and settle for less than the amount owed. And you'll learn how to improve your chances of actually cashing in on a small claims court judgment. You'll not only be counseled on the selection of collection agencies and collection attorneys, but you'll learn the importance of protecting yourself from the collection agencies and collection attorneys you ultimately choose. You'll also be shown how to control costs and monitor the effectiveness of third-party debt collectors. Finally, you'll be introduced to a nonjudicial form of dispute resolution known as ADR. With the ever-increasing logjam of cases clogging up the nation's judicial system, ADR holds great promise as a logical alternative to adversary proceedings, which often leave everyone—except the attorneys—angry, tired, and broke.

This book will also help you if:

1. You're interested in making the most of your precious time.
2. You're looking for ideas to energize a tired credit and collection staff.
3. You want to increase cooperation between your sales force and your credit department.
4. You're tired of borrowing money at high interest rates to cover delinquent receivables.
5. You're not sure what to say when someone calls you for a credit reference.
6. You need help but don't know where to turn.

Regardless of the financial condition, level of sophistication, or size of your company, this book will boost your confidence, sharpen your skills, and heighten your understanding of the credit process. It may even save your neck!

Remember, of course, that the information in *Turning Debts into Dollars* is general in nature. Before implementing any of the procedures covered in the book I advise you to consult with your attorney, business adviser, or credit and collection consultant.

PART I. CREDIT-GRANTING STRATEGY

Before writing this book I spoke with office managers, attorneys, company owners, administrative assistants, company presidents, sales managers, bank supervisors, and business leaders of all kinds. These people all had one thing in common: they wanted to know how to control their receivables. I also solicited input from a number of distinguished credit managers. Although they agreed that the business community needs credit and collection advice, education, and training, most of these credit professionals were skeptical of the readiness, willingness, and ability of business people to confront the issue of receivable control.

The more I thought about it, the more this apparent inconsistency bothered me. How could the business community's obvious hunger for loss-limiting advice be reconciled with the perception among trained credit professionals that businesses couldn't care less about credit management? Knowing that business people do want to learn more about credit granting and debt collecting, it occurred to me that somehow the professional credit management fraternity had lost touch with the concerns and needs of those who make most of the credit and collection decisions in this country—the nonprofessional credit people.

You don't have to look far for a specific example. Most of the receivable-control manuals on the market discuss the importance of obtaining audited financial statements from businesses and detailed credit histories from consumers before extending credit. While it would be helpful to see such information before extending credit, the facts indicate that few credit granters ever do.

A purely theoretical approach to credit granting may look good on paper, but it won't help the average small business control receivables. Credit granters must focus on what is practical, workable, and doable. One should also remember that most small companies are not staffed by trained credit professionals. The responsibility for credit decisions is often delegated to persons who neither have the time nor the desire to learn everything there is to know about credit management. They simply need to know how they can do a better job, use their time more productively, and find help when something goes awry.

Even companies with professional credit managers are faced with the hard realities of business, however. Small companies, new companies, and companies operating in highly competitive business environments routinely accept more risk than large, established, secure companies. Company policy considerations always precede credit policy considerations. You've got to fit credit control into the way you do business, not the other way around.

Having observed, participated in, and advised small businesses of all kinds, I've had a chance to see what the average small business faces. I know that many companies are reluctant to control receivables because they're afraid it will cost them time, money, business, or all three. That is because no one has ever explained to them the value of relatively simple, inexpensive credit control techniques. Remember Wolner's Rule: *Before you can solve a really big problem, you've got to solve all the little problems that created it.*

My theme is back to basics. You don't need to be a financial wizard or a Harvard graduate to extend credit. You do need to be aware, informed, and self-assured. You'll never find a fail-safe plan to insure credit-granting success, nor a surefire way to avoid credit loss. If you expect this book to provide either of the above, read no further. But if you want this book to provide a blueprint for credit-granting success, read on. You are certain to gain insight into credit granting.

As we talk more specifically about extending credit, I do want to go on record as rejecting the pessimism of many of my professional credit colleagues. My faith in the ability of the business community to accept, learn from, and effectively use common sense techniques, like those contained in this book, is unshaken.

CHAPTER 1
FACTORS AFFECTING YOUR STRATEGY

Most books of this kind start by tracing the historical beginnings of credit and explaining the modern-day boom in consumer and commercial credit. This book doesn't. Instead, it begins by examining the primary factors that are likely to shape your overall approach to credit granting. These are the four factors that will determine your credit-granting strategy: (1) your reasons for extending credit; (2) your company credit and sales philosophy; (3) your available resources to screen credit applicants and collect past-due accounts; and (4) your past success or lack of success in controlling receivables.

REASONS FOR EXTENDING CREDIT

There are a number of reasons why companies offer credit terms to their customers:

1. Competition—You're doing it to meet or beat the competition. If you're in a competitive industry, getting more business may mean offering customers a better deal. If the competition owns a commanding share of the market and offers customers credit terms, you may be forced to offer more attractive credit terms.
2. Customer convenience—You're doing it to earn the loyalty of your customers. You may feel that allowing your customers to charge it is the best way to boost customer goodwill.
3. Increase sales—You're doing it to expand sales. Perhaps you've got excess manufacturing capacity, an inventory buildup, or a profit margin so slim that you need to generate additional sales. A higher volume of credit sales may be the only answer.
4. Establish new accounts—You're doing it to get noticed. If the competition doesn't offer credit terms to prospective customers, you probably will to get a shot at their business.

5. Capitalize on general economic conditions—You're doing it to make up for lost time. Companies often compensate for decreased sales during recessionary times by expanding credit sales during prosperous times.

If you offer credit terms, you're probably doing it for one or more of these reasons.

COMPANY CREDIT AND SALES PHILOSOPHY

Your company's philosophy concerning credit sales will also have a major impact on your credit-granting strategy. Companies typically fall within one of the following categories:

1. Primitive—Companies in this classification usually grant unlimited credit to anyone requesting it, without asking for or verifying any credit data. These are desperate companies.
2. Elementary—Companies in this classification usually grant credit in substantial amounts, requesting only sketchy credit information and without conducting any credit investigation.
3. Advanced—Companies in this classification usually grant credit in modest amounts to those who agree to provide a limited amount of verifiable credit information. They reserve credit investigations for large-dollar transactions.
4. More advanced—Companies in this classification usually grant credit in nominal amounts to those who provide a full credit history. They conduct limited credit investigations on every account and full-scale investigations (including the verification of references) on large-dollar transactions.
5. Sophisticated—Companies in this classification seldom grant credit on initial orders except to established, well-known firms. All potential customers are required to submit a full credit history with financial information, a financial statement, or both. Full credit investigations are conducted on every new account (including reports from credit reporting agencies and verification of references), and existing customers are periodically reevaluated.

Your company philosophy toward credit sales will also be affected by the normal changes that accompany growth and development. Your credit-granting strategy will change as your company progresses through the various stages of its life cycle.

Most companies start out hungry for business. To become better known their credit terms may be quite liberal. Credit sales are better than no sales at all. As a company grows, its approach to credit granting may become more cautious. With a larger number of customers to choose from there is less reason to go after the riskier business. After achieving success and establishing a solid customer base, companies often move toward even more restrictive credit policies. Successful companies can afford to make their own rules. Eventually, established companies experience competition from newer, hungrier companies. When this happens a more liberal credit policy may be needed to keep customers from straying.

COMPANY RESOURCES

Your company's resources or lack of them will have a major impact on your credit-granting strategy. The more careful you are in qualifying or screening your credit customers, the less time you will have to spend collecting—and vice versa. If you lack sufficient resources to either check out or follow up on your credit customers you could have trouble, especially if the nature of your business allows no choice but to sell on credit.

There are four prime considerations:

1. Time—checking references, processing credit applications, setting up new accounts—everything in the process of extending credit takes time. If you knowingly sell to struggling companies or you have a very liberal credit policy, you must be prepared to allocate additional time to collect your money.
2. Money—credit reports, telephone calls, postage stamps, salaries, wages, and equipment cost money. The amount of money you spend screening credit applicants will depend on the level of risk you are exposed to and your ability to absorb expected losses.
3. Technology—depending on your company's size and sales volume, you may need sophisticated telecommunications equipment, computer terminals, or other devices to gather, store, and retrieve data. The key to credit granting is effective information management. The less able you are to manage information, the less likely you are to ask for it and the less likely you will be to make use of it if you do get it.
4. Personnel—regardless of company size, you must have an adequate workforce to manage the credit-granting process. If

you lack the personnel to properly screen credit applicants, you must be prepared to add to your collection staff or retain the services of a third-party debt collector, such as a collection agency or attorney.

It is necessary to put credit-granting expenditures into proper perspective. Credit extending is a risky proposition. The allocation of resources to control credit losses should be considered an investment in the financial health of your company. This is especially true if you are dependent on borrowed funds or are short of working capital.

PAST SUCCESS IN CONTROLLING RECEIVABLES

Have your past efforts to control receivables been effective? Your answer to that question will have a major effect on your credit-granting strategy. No matter what you're currently doing to screen credit applicants, you'll have to do more if your receivables are on the rise. If, however, your current efforts seem to be working, you won't want to make major changes.

To determine whether your credit-granting strategy is working, you must have some way to gauge its effectiveness. One of the most common indicators of credit and collection efficiency is the Days' Sales Outstanding (D.S.O.) formula:

$$\text{D.S.O.} = \frac{\text{Current End of Month A/R Balance} \times 90}{\text{Total Sales for Past 3 Months}}$$

By multiplying your current end of month receivables balance by 90 and dividing that number by total sales for the past 3 months, you end up with the number of days' sales outstanding. For example, assume your current end of month receivables are $12,000 and that your total sales for the past 3 months are $30,000 ($10,000 each month). Using the D.S.O. formula the result would be:

$$\frac{\$12,000 \times 90}{\$30,000} = \text{D.S.O. of 36 days}$$

Stated another way, D.S.O. is an indication of the length of time it would take you to sell enough to match the amount of receivables on your books. If your customers are expected to pay within thirty days, your D.S.O. should be as close to thirty days as possible.

A more precise way to measure the age of receivables uses a formula known as Dollar Days Outstanding (D.D.O.). To determine your D.D.O. you must: (1) multiply the face amount of each invoice by its actual age in days to determine the "dollar days" for each invoice; (2) add the dollar days of all the outstanding invoices together to determine the total dollar days; and (3) divide the total dollar days by the total dollar amount of all outstanding invoices. See figure 1.

Your credit-granting strategy must be flexible enough to adapt to changing conditions. Because things can and do change very quickly, it's dangerous to be complacent.

OTHER ELEMENTS

There are other elements that have an impact on your credit-granting strategy other than your company philosophy concerning credit sales, your credit management resources, and your past success (or lack of it) in controlling receivables. We have already discussed elements like your profit margin, your willingness and ability to manage receivables, the fiscal stability of your company, the amount of competition you face, and the financial health of the businesses and industries you serve.

Your credit-granting strategy will be largely shaped by elements beyond your control. While some companies seem to have an easy time of it, others are constantly struggling. There are ways to tip the odds in your favor, however, and many are amazingly simple and inexpensive to implement.

FIGURE 1
CALCULATING DOLLAR DAYS OUTSTANDING*

The following chart represents the accounts receivable aging for a hypothetical company, the Acme Secretarial Service of Minneapolis, Minnesota.

0-29	30-59	60-89	90+	TOTAL
2550	270	250	80	
2250	240	200	75	
1575	190	150	60	
1250	170	100	35	
1000	130	50		
750				
450				
175				
$10,000	$1,000	$750	$250	$12,000

Sales: $10,000 — Terms: Net 30 Days — D.S.O.: 36 Days

While Dollar Days Outstanding (D.D.O.) is a much more precise measure of the age of receivables than D.S.O., the calculations are a bit complicated. For that reason, companies without computerized accounts receivable agings would find it burdensome to use D.D.O. If, on the other hand, your company has access to computerized aging information, determining D.D.O. would be a relatively simple matter.

As an example, however, let's determine the D.D.O. for this company the old-fashioned way. We'll start by calculating the

---

*Reprinted with permission from *Credit & Financial Management*, copyright © 1983, published by the National Association of Credit Management, 475 Park Avenue South, New York, N.Y. 10016. Adapted from the article by Robert W. Eichorn, "Dollar Days Outstanding," January 1983.

D.D.O. for each receivable category. To do that multiply each outstanding invoice by the specific number of days it has been outstanding to determine the number of dollar days. Then add up the dollar days for each outstanding invoice to get the total number of dollar days in each receivable category. Finally, divide the total number of dollar days by the total dollar amount of the invoices in the category.

Current (less than 30 days)

Amount Due	Age in Days	Dollar Days
$ 2,550	28	71,400
$ 2,250	25	56,250
$ 1,575	20	31,500
$ 1,250	15	18,750
$ 1,000	11	11,000
$ 750	9	6,750
$ 450	8	3,600
$ 175	5	875
$10,000		200,125

$$\frac{200,125}{10,000} = 20.01 \text{ D.D.O.}$$

30 Days

Amount Due	Age in Days	Dollar Days
$ 270	57	15,390
$ 240	51	12,240
$ 190	44	8,360
$ 170	37	6,290
$ 130	32	4,160
$ 1,000		46,440

$$\frac{46,440}{1,000} = 46.44 \text{ D.D.O.}$$

60 Days

Amount Due	Age in Days	Dollar Days
$ 250	82	20,500
$ 200	75	15,000
$ 150	70	10,500
$ 100	68	6,800
$ 50	62	3,100
$ 750		55,900

$55,900 / $750 = 74.53 D.D.O.

90 Days (and over)

Amount Due	Age in Days	Dollar Days
$ 80	180	14,400
$ 75	150	11,250
$ 60	120	7,200
$ 35	105	3,675
$ 250		36,525

$36,525 / $250 = 146.10 D.D.O.

The D.D.O. for each aging category tells us precisely how many days the invoices in each category have been outstanding. As you can see, some invoices in the current category are less current than others. The same is true for invoices in the other aging categories as well.

You may also wish to calculate the overall number of delinquent dollar days outstanding. To do that add up the number of dollar days in each of the delinquent categories and divide by the total dollar amount of the delinquent invoices.

```
 46,440   30-Day Dollar Days
 55,900   60-Day Dollar Days
 36,525   90+-Day Dollar Days
138,865   Total Delinquent Dollar Days
$2,000 = 69.43 Delinquent Dollar Days Outstanding
```

To determine the overall dollar days add the current dollar days and the delinquent dollar days together and divide by the total dollar amount of all oustanding invoices.

```
200,125   Current Dollar Days
138,865   Delinquent Dollar Days
338,990   Total Dollar Days
$12,000 = 28.25 Total Dollar Days Outstanding
```

CHAPTER 2
SELECTING A STRATEGY

Your next task is to select the credit-granting strategy you intend to use. Most companies find it somewhat difficult to decide on a credit-granting strategy. A tough, rigid approach to credit-granting may adversely affect sales. A weak, inconsistent approach may lead to credit losses. How do you decide what's right for your company? Ask yourself three important questions:

1. Is your credit policy acceptable to your customers? Customer acceptance is affected by a number of things—the credit terms your customers are accustomed to, whether your customers are able to obtain the same product or service from other suppliers, and the demand for your product or service.
   New companies, companies operating in competitive business environments, and companies trying to introduce new product lines must guard against implementing overly restrictive credit procedures. Becoming established and winning business from the competition requires caution and moderation. You should compare the number of orders you accept with the number of orders you reject. If you find yourself turning down more and more orders, or large numbers of interested prospects seem to be walking out without ordering, your credit-granting strategy may be too strict. If you seldom turn down an order, your credit-granting strategy may be too lenient.*

---

*If it appears that your approach to credit granting is too lenient, you'll want to make a change. Remember that it will take your established customers awhile to adjust to a more restrictive credit policy (sixty to ninety days is average). You may even experience a temporary decrease in sales. Eventually things will return to normal if you have explained to your customers why the change was necessary (to avoid price increases by

2. Are you serious about enforcing the terms of your credit policy? Does your credit policy stand for something? Or are your customers allowed to violate it with impunity?

   You must earn the respect of your customers by being firm but flexible. You might encounter situations that warrant a departure from your normal credit policy. But you must be careful. Offering substantially different credit terms to customers who meet similar creditworthiness standards is a form of illegal discrimination. (For a discussion of the legal aspects of consumer and commercial credit granting, see Part I, chapter three).

3. Is there support within your organization for your credit-granting strategy? The people within your company must be comfortable with your approach to credit granting. Your strategy must be perceived as consistent with the goals and objectives of your company. The support of your credit department is essential to the success of your credit-granting strategy. Winning support, however, means providing credit employees with sufficient training, supervision, motivation, and resources to get the job done.

   The support of upper management is just as important. If management frequently overturns decisions made by the credit department, your credit-granting strategy could be in jeopardy. Erosion of credit department authority destroys the morale of credit employees, negatively affects the company's ability to control receivables, and hampers the ability of customers to understand and comply with your credit policy.

   The support of the people in your sales department is also crucial, as is the support of those in other departments directly or indirectly involved in administering, explaining, or resolving credit matters. To win support it is usually necessary to provide noncredit personnel with enough information to demonstrate how and why your credit-granting strategy is beneficial to the employees, customers, and company as a whole.

---

holding the line on bad-debt losses, for example). If substantial resistance persists beyond ninety days, you should examine your new credit policy more closely.

CHAPTER 3
GETTING TO KNOW PROSPECTIVE CUSTOMERS

Gathering credit information is one of the most crucial tasks a company must perform. Every creditor needs to get to know prospective credit customers. To do so, you'll need to get answers to questions that bear on the creditworthiness of your prospects.

In this chapter four major credit information sources will be discussed: (1) credit applications, (2) trade references, (3) bank references, and (4) civic, credit, and trade associations.

CREDIT APPLICATIONS

The most common way to gather credit information is by asking your customer to fill out a credit application. See figures 2 and 3 for examples of credit application forms.

A credit application has two main purposes. The first is to gather information that will help you decide whether to extend credit. The second is to gather information that may help you enforce your credit policy after you have decided to extend credit.

Credit applications also have several secondary purposes. Many companies write their credit terms into the credit application forms they use. The applicant is then required to confirm acceptance of those terms by signing a statement similar to this: "My signature indicates that I understand and agree to comply fully with the terms and conditions enumerated in this credit application." It is also wise to include in every credit application a veracity clause that might say, for example: "My signature certifies that everything I have stated in this application is correct to the best of my knowledge."

Some credit granters think of credit applications as nuisances. But every company needs a certain amount of credit information. Some credit granters are afraid to ask for completed credit applications because they're concerned about offending potential customers.

FIGURE 2A
COMMERCIAL CREDIT APPLICATION

HARMON GLASS COMPANY APPLICATION FOR CREDIT
4000 Olson Memorial Highway, Minneapolis, MN 55422
FAX: 612-520-0798 ♦ PHONE: 612-520-0656

The "Undersigned" hereby makes this application for credit to the HARMON GLASS COMPANY, ("Creditor"), and in making this application the Undersigned agrees that all amounts shall be paid within the Creditor's Net 10th Prox terms, and if not paid according to said terms, are then delinquent. The Undersigned agrees to pay 18% per annum on all invoices 30 days or more past due. Should a credit availability be granted by Creditor, all decisions with respect to the extension or continuation of credit shall be at sole discretion of Creditor. Creditor may terminate any credit availability within its sole discretion. The Undersigned shall be responsible for all collection costs and attorney's fees in connection with any delinquent amount.

LEGAL NAME OF BUSINESS: _____ DATE: _____

STREET ADDRESS OF BUSINESS: _____
                                                                                                City   State   Zip
MAILING ADDRESS (if different from street address): _____
                                                                                                City   State   Zip
PHONE: (____)_____ FAX: (____)_____

CHECK LEGAL STATUS (√): Corporation _____ Proprietorship _____ Partnership _____ Limited Partnership _____
STATE OF INCORPORATION OR REGISTRATION OF PARTNERSHIP: _____
CHECK HERE IF INCORPORATED WITHIN THE LAST TWELVE MONTHS (√): _____
CHECK HERE IF CASH SALES ARE OKAY UNTIL CREDIT AVAILABILITY HAS BEEN DETERMINED (√): _____

LIST ALL OWNERS, PARTNERS, OR CORPORATE OFFICERS (Please include titles and social security numbers):

Name	City, State	Phone	Title	Social Security Number

ATTACHED TO THIS CREDIT APPLICATION IS THE MOST RECENT FINANCIAL STATEMENT OF THE UNDERSIGNED. *The Undersigned agrees to provide updated financial information to Creditor on request, and to provide an annual financial statement to Creditor as a condition of the continuation of credit. The Undersigned agrees to provide an updated credit application to Creditor each year as a condition for the continued extension of credit.*

The following is a list of all creditors of the Undersigned who hold liens or security interests in assets of the Undersigned (Please list name of creditor, brief description of secured assets, and amount of debt):

_____
_____

BANK REFERENCE:

Bank	Bank Address		
Bank officer or department		Checking or Savings Account Number	Loan Number

TRADE REFERENCES:

	Business Name	Complete Address	Phone
1.			
2.			
3.			

THE PARTIES HERETO KNOWINGLY AND INTENTIONALLY WAIVE THE RIGHT TO A JURY TRIAL ON ANY ISSUE OR DISPUTE THAT MAY ARISE BETWEEN THEM. **TERMS AND CONDITIONS OF SALE:** *The Undersigned agrees to pay for all purchases according to the Creditor's Net 10th Prox terms. No terms or conditions of purchase orders different from the terms of Creditor will become part of any sales agreement, purchase order, or other document unless specifically approved in writing by Creditor. The Undersigned agrees that its continued solvency is a precondition of any sale made by Creditor. The undersigned agrees to provide a statement to Creditor on request representing that the Undersigned is and remains solvent. The Undersigned acknowledges and agrees that Creditor may utilize outside credit reporting services and investigate references listed to obtain information on the Undersigned. The Undersigned grants to the Creditor a security interest in undersigned's equipment, contract rights, inventories, receivables and proceeds of sales as collateral to secure the Undersigned's performance of all obligations. The Undersigned further authorizes the Creditor to file a financing statement without Undersigned's signature. The laws of the State of Minnesota shall be applicable to all suits arising under any agreement between the Undersigned and the Creditor. All accounts shall be due and payable in Minneapolis, Minnesota. In the event of litigation, venue shall be in Minneapolis, Minnesota.*

THE PERSON SIGNING THIS APPLICATION CERTIFIES THAT ALL INFORMATION CONTAINED IN THIS APPLICATION (AND ANY ATTACHMENTS) IS TRUE TO THE BEST OF THEIR KNOWLEDGE AND BELIEF.

_____   _____
Signature of Owner/Partner/President   Printed or Typed Name of Owner/Partner/President

FIGURE 2B
COMMERCIAL CREDIT APPLICATION

(This form approved and published by the National Association of Credit Management)

APPLICATION FOR CREDIT

Date _____ 19 _____

ISSUED TO _____ Name of FIRM Requesting Statement

(PLEASE ANSWER ALL QUESTIONS. WHEN NO FIGURES ARE INSERTED, WRITE WORD "NONE")

FIRM NAME	TRADE STYLE		
STREET ADDRESS		PHONE	
CITY	STATE		ZIP CODE

FULL NAME OF OWNER OR OWNERS (OR AN AUTHORIZED OFFICER OF CORPORATION). LIST HOME ADDRESS & ZIP CODE FOR PARTNERSHIP OR INDIVIDUAL.

PLEASE CHECK ONE	INDIVIDUAL	PARTNERSHIP	CORPORATION	FED. TAX NO. (FOR CORPORATION)	MARITAL STATUS

ADDITIONAL INFORMATION REQUIRED FOR CONDITIONAL SALES CONTRACTS UNDER THE UNIFORM COMMERCIAL CODE

DEBTOR (INDIVIDUAL SIGNING CONTRACT) _____ TITLE: _____

DEBTOR'S SOCIAL SECURITY NO. (FOR PARTNERSHIP OR INDIVIDUAL) _____

TYPE OF BUSINESS		DATE STARTED
ESTIMATED ANNUAL SALES		
FORMER BUSINESS	LOCATION	
OWN OR RENT BUILDING — IF RENT — FROM WHOM?		VALUE
REAL ESTATE MORTGAGE		

TRADE REFERENCES

NAME	ADDRESS

NAME OF BANK	ACCOUNT NO.
STREET ADDRESS	
CITY	STATE

Arbitration Agreement: The parties agree to resolve by binding arbitration all claims and disputes arising from or relating to agreements and transactions, including the validity of this arbitration clause. The arbitration shall be governed by the Code of Procedure of Equilaw's National Arbitration Forum (NAF). The applicable Code shall be the Code of Procedure in effect at the time the claim is filed with Equilaw, whose United States administrative office is located at 2124 Dupont Avenue South, Minneapolis, Minnesota 55405, (612) 871-9205. The parties agree to accept service by certified mail, return receipt requested, through the United States Postal Service, of the Initial Claim Documents which begin an arbitration. Judgment upon the Award may be entered in any court having jurisdiction.

THE ABOVE INFORMATION AS WELL AS THAT GIVEN ON THE REVERSE SIDE IS FOR THE PURPOSE OF OBTAINING CREDIT AND IS WARRANTED TO BE TRUE. I/WE HEREBY AUTHORIZE THE FIRM TO WHOM THIS APPLICATION IS MADE TO INVESTIGATE THE REFERENCES LISTED PERTAINING TO MY/OUR CREDIT AND FINANCIAL RESPONSIBILITY.

APPLICANT'S SIGNATURE ATTESTS FINANCIAL RESPONSI-BILITY, ABILITY AND WILLINGNESS TO PAY OUR INVOICES IN ACCORDANCE WITH FOLLOWING TERMS:

FIRM NAME _____

BY _____ TITLE _____

BY _____ TITLE _____

Printed In The U.S.A.

FIGURE 3
CONSUMER CREDIT APPLICATION

CREDIT APPLICATION

Please indicate below name in which account is to be carried. Applicant, if married, may apply for a separate account.

Name (First)_____(Middle Initial)_____(Last)_____

Social Security Number _____ Date of Birth_____ Number of Dependents_____

Home Address (Street)_____(City)_____(State)____(Zip Code)_____

Home Phone (   )_____ Education Completed ❑ High School ❑ College ❑ Graduate School

Previous address (if less than 1 year at present address)

(Street)_____(City)_____(State)_____(Zip Code)_____

Monthly Rent/Mortgage Amount ❑ Rent ❑ Own   Annual Income *
$_____ How Long at Present Address_____ $_____

*Alimony, child support or separate maintenance income need not be revealed if I do not wish to have it considered as a basis for repaying this obligation.

Other income $_____ Source _____

Name of individual for additional income verification _____

Address _____ City _____

Employer_____Title/Position_____

City of Employer_____ State_____ Zip Code_____ Self Employed ❑ Yes ❑ No

Business Phone (   )_____ Length of Employment (Years)_____(Months)_____

Previous Employer _____ State_____ Zip Code_____

Banking Relationships

Bank Name_____ City/State_____ ❑ Checking ❑ Savings

Bank Name_____ City/State_____ ❑ Checking ❑ Savings

Spouse information to be completed if: (1) Your spouse is an authorized buyer, (2) You reside in a community property state (AZ,CA,ID, LA, NV, NM, TX, WA, WI), or (3) You are relying on the income or assets of a spouse as a source for payment.

Spouse Name (First)_____ _____(Middle Initial)_____(Last)_____

Social Security Number _____ Date of Birth _____

Employer _____ Business Phone _____

Applicant's Signature**_____ Date_____

**By signing, I ask that an account be opened for me, and I certify that everthing I have stated in this Application is correct to the best of my knowledge. I agree to be bound by the terms of the Agreement to be provided to me and the terms of this Application.

Fortunately, people seeking credit now expect to be asked to fill out credit applications.

There are five questions you should ask yourself about the credit application form you intend to use:

1. Does it ask the questions I most want answered?
2. Are my customers ready, willing, and able to provide the information I have requested?
3. Have I made it as convenient as possible for the customer to provide the information?
4. Does the customer understand why I need the information and how I intend to use it?
5. Is it legal? This question is particularly important if you're involved in consumer credit transactions.

You can buy credit application forms in any office supply store, but preprinted forms may not meet your needs. I suggest buying single copies of several commercially prepared forms to use as a guide in drafting your own credit application. If the commercially prepared forms you obtain call for more information than you need, select the questions you most want answered and disregard the rest.*

Consumer Credit Applications

If you sell a product or service to an individual—a consumer—and that product or service is intended for that individual's personal use, you're involved in consumer credit. That creditors need information about the individuals to whom they extend credit has already been established. But a myriad of local, state, and federal consumer protection laws make acquiring such information a tricky proposition. Credit granters do have the right to determine if credit applicants are creditworthy, and that generally means asking for basic credit information.

For small-dollar consumer credit transactions you will want to know:

---

*You are cautioned against adding questions of your own to consumer credit applications until you have consulted with an attorney. There are certain questions credit granters are not allowed to ask consumers.

1. The applicant's full name;
2. Current address and previous address if the applicant has been at the current address less than one year;
3. Current phone number, if any;
4. Current employer, including address and phone number and previous employer if the applicant has been with the current employer less than one year, and the nature of the position held;
5. A driver's license number, social security number, or both.

If the transaction involves a substantial amount of money, you should obtain the following additional information:

6. The name, address, and account number of the applicant's bank, plus the length of time the account has been maintained;
7. The name, address, and telephone number of the applicant's nearest relative or close friend;
8. The names, addresses, and telephone numbers of several trade references;
9. The applicant's monthly income and an estimate of the applicant's monthly expenses.

Under the terms of the Equal Credit Opportunity Act, you may not request the marital status of a person applying for an individual, unsecured account.* You do, however, have the right to ask whether the account is going to be an individual or a joint account. If it is a joint account, you may request the applicant's marital status, but you are only entitled to know if the applicant is married, unmarried, or separated. The term *unmarried* applies to single, widowed, and divorced people.

Under no circumstances is it permissible for a creditor to deny credit based on marital status. Similarly, credit applicants are not obligated to divulge income resulting from welfare, alimony, or child support, unless the applicant chooses to disclose such income voluntarily to improve the chances of getting credit.

---

*This is true in all but the following community property states: Arizona, California, Idaho, Louisiana, Nevada, New Mexico, Texas, and Washington.

Federal legislation governs much of what credit granters do when seeking and handling credit information. The Equal Credit Opportunity Act prohibits discrimination against applicants on the basis of sex, marital status, race, color, religion, national origin, age, and certain other factors. See appendix B. Another federal law, the Fair Credit Reporting Act, gives credit applicants the right to get a summary of their credit history from a credit-reporting agency and to correct inaccurate information contained therein. See appendix C. The Fair Credit Reporting Act also gives the credit applicant the right to request a written explanation of the reason for a credit denial when it is based on information from a source other than a credit-reporting agency. While the Fair Credit Reporting Act does not require credit granters to divulge their information sources, it does require the release of enough information to afford the applicant an opportunity to challenge the accuracy of the data.

Commercial Credit Applications

If you sell to a company or individual a product or service that has a business purpose, you're involved in commercial credit. While there are fewer restrictions governing commercial credit transactions, the amounts of money involved are normally larger and the risks much greater than those associated with consumer transactions. For that reason commercial credit granters must ask special questions to protect themselves. Commercial creditors need to know:

1. The company's legal name. This is the name officially registered with the state and county in which the company does business;
2. The names, addresses and social security numbers of the principals of the company;
3. The company's address, the length of time there and the previous address if at the current location less than one year;
4. The length of time the company has been in business;
5. The name of the company's bank (address, type of account, account number, and duration of the banking relationship);
6. The names, addresses, and phone numbers of trade references;
7. The type of product or service the company supplies;
8. The legal status of the company.

A *sole proprietorship* is defined as an individual engaged in business who is personally responsible for debts incurred by the business. The business and personal assets of the proprietor are available to creditors for the payment of the proprietorship's debts.

A *partnership* is defined as two or more individuals engaged in business who are jointly responsible for debts incurred by the business. The business and personal assets of the principal partners are available to creditors for the payment of the partnership's debts.

A *corporation* is defined as one or more individuals engaged in business who have been granted special legal status and who are insulated from personal responsibility for corporate debts. Only corporate assets are available to creditors for the payment of the corporation's debts.*

Other Considerations

There are a few other things to remember about credit applications:

1. If possible, advise credit applicants in advance that you'll need to know names, addresses, telephone numbers, account numbers, and so forth so that they can locate the necessary information before filling out your credit application. What should you do if the applicant is ready to buy but isn't able to provide all the information you need to make a decision? First, take the order. Then advise the customer that you will hold the order pending receipt of the requested information and completion of your credit investigation.
2. Simplify your credit application forms. Ask only for the information you really need to make a decision. Make it clear, however, that you expect answers to the questions you do ask. This is especially important if noncredit personnel—salespeople or other field representatives, for example—are responsible for getting your credit applications completed. If credit applicants skip certain questions, ask them for an explanation on the spot. Remember Wolner's Rule: *Get all the information you need the first time around. What you don't know can hurt you.*

---

*An officer or director of a corporation could be held personally responsible for corporate debts if he or she provides a personal guarantee. It is not unusual for credit granters to seek personal guarantees when dealing with new or financially troubled corporations.

3. Periodically update the credit applications you have on file. Since things seldom stay the same, it's dangerous to rely on old information. If you deal with companies in stable industries, a yearly review is probably sufficient. If you deal with companies in volatile industries, a quarterly or semiannual review is advised.
4. Take the time to check out the credit applications you receive. It's not necessary to conduct a full-scale investigation of every credit applicant, but it is important to have confidence in the integrity of the information you have gathered.

TRADE REFERENCES

There are three things you need to know about trade references: (1) when you should verify trade credit information; (2) the circumstances under which credit granters are entitled to obtain trade credit information from other credit granters; and (3) the form your request for trade credit information should take.

Verifying Trade Credit Information

Creditors seldom verify all the trade references listed by credit applicants on their credit applications. In fact, some creditors never verify trade references. Whether you decide to check trade references or not depends on several factors:

1. The volume of credit applications you process. If you process a large volume of credit applications you may not have time to thoroughly check trade references.
2. The dollar amounts of the credit transactions involved. If a lot of money is involved, you'll be more willing to check references.
3. The accessibility of the information. If you're able to get the information you need over the telephone, you'll be more likely to ask for it than if it's necessary to submit a written request.
4. The amount of time you have to make a credit decision. If you're required to decide quickly, you may not have sufficient time to contact trade references.
5. The demeanor of the applicant. If the applicant acts suspiciously, you'll be more inclined to check references.

Ideally, it would be best to routinely check all references. Unfortunately, most companies check references only when large amounts of money are involved or when the applicant acts suspiciously. Many credit granters view reference checking as a waste of time because they assume all credit applicants provide their three best references. Why would anyone give a credit granter a poor or nonexistent credit reference?

Not all credit applicants have acceptable credit references. Some credit applicants figure they've got nothing to lose and everything to gain by listing poor or nonexistent credit references. Despite the risks, however, many companies just don't have the time, money, and personnel to check every credit reference.

What should you do if you're in this category? First, advise all credit applicants—before you ask them to fill out a credit application—that you routinely check credit references. If you confront the issue head-on, credit applicants are likely to think twice about giving you false or misleading information. Saying that you routinely check credit references doesn't obligate you to contact every credit reference, but it puts credit applicants on notice that you might.

Second, spot check your credit applications. If you don't have time to contact every credit reference, get in touch with as many as possible. Don't forget to verify the names, addresses, and phone numbers of the references listed.

Right to Trade Credit Information

Only people with legitimate reasons for seeking trade credit information should be allowed to obtain it. Similarly, people who are in a position to provide trade credit information are obligated to determine whether requests for such information are legitimate.

Persons initiating credit inquiries should be asked to identify themselves, their company, and the reason for the request. Examples of legitimate reasons for obtaining trade credit information include routine credit checks, credit application verifications, credit limit determinations, and credit file updates. If you are asked for trade credit information and you have doubts about the identity of the person making the request or about the legitimacy of the request, you should refuse to provide any credit information.

When handling telephone credit inquiries you are advised to get the name and phone number of the caller and offer to call the person back. Never disclose credit information until you are sure of the caller's identity. Then, if everything checks out, call the person back and provide the information. If you still have doubts, simply ask the caller to put the request in writing.

Form of Request

It's not always easy to obtain trade credit information when you need it. Companies are increasingly reluctant to provide trade credit information over the telephone. While you may have a few close associates who will honor your telephone requests, you'll more often have to put your requests in writing.

Whether you ask for trade credit information by telephone or letter, however, there are two things you must do before doing anything else. First, make it clear to providers of trade credit information that you will keep such information confidential.* Second, you should offer to reciprocate. Because responding to a request for trade credit information is an inconvenience, it is often helpful to let the other creditors know you'll be happy to return the favor should they need similar information from you.

Rights of Inquiry

Generally, you should not expect to get information from another creditor that you wouldn't be willing to provide yourself. If you are called on to provide information about a credit customer, only factual, verifiable ledger experience should be disclosed. Irrelevant and unsubstantiated observations concerning the personality and personal habits of the credit customer should not be interjected.

What if damaging information of a personal nature is disclosed to you during a credit inquiry? Should you include such information in your credit file or consider it when making a credit granting decision? The answer to both questions is "no." The only information your credit file should contain and the only information you should consider when making a credit-granting decision is information that bears directly on the creditworthiness of the applicant.

Why shouldn't you include information of a personal nature in your credit file if it is given to you? One reason is that it could be dangerous to include unproven information in your credit files. If

---

*If you're obtaining consumer credit information, however, you should seek permission to disclose the identity of the source of the information and relevant details concerning the information to the subject of the information. You should also make it clear that such information will be disclosed only if the subject of the information asks you to do so.

someone with access to your credit files inadvertently discloses such information to a third party you could be in trouble, especially if the information is disclosed to another credit granter and is used to deny credit to the subject of the information. Another reason is that unsubstantiated information is meaningless unless you're able to confirm it. Furthermore, when it comes to determining creditworthiness, the only thing that matters is whether people are likely to pay their bills on time.

What types of questions are legitimate when answering or initiating a credit inquiry?

1. Current balance—The current balance owing on an account is relevant to any credit inquiry. It is crucial, however, for providers of credit information to disclose exactly when the balance was last updated and the length of time it normally takes to process payments.
2. High credit during last twelve months—Creditors need to know what the maximum credit exposure has been at any one time during the preceding year.
3. Current account status—Is the account up-to-date or past-due? If the account is past-due, you should be specific about the exact number of days the account is past-due. Once again, it's important to disclose how current your information is.
4. Normal account terms—People seeking credit information need to know what your normal terms are. Other creditors will be interested in the length of time you allow accounts to go unpaid before you consider them past-due.

There are two other questions that frequently come up. Both should be handled with the utmost caution. First, if the trade reference reports a past-due balance, does the past-due balance result from an unresolved dispute? Second, does the customer normally pay on time? Let's discuss each of these questions separately:

1. Is the customer delaying payment because of an unresolved dispute? If your customer has alerted you to a dispute and is withholding payment pending resolution of the dispute, you are obliged to report that fact when responding to a credit inquiry. It is important for every credit granter to design a procedure for identifying and resolving disputed accounts. Identifying a customer as past-due without explaining all the relevant details

during a credit inquiry would be highly improper. In the case of a consumer credit transaction and presuming the creditor was properly notified under the provisions of yet another federal law, the Fair Credit Billing Act, such an omission would be illegal. See appendix D.
2. Does the customer normally pay on time? This could be a tricky question. It is often impossible to generalize when categorizing a customer's payment habits because people don't always pay consistently. You are advised not to generalize about a customer's payment record unless you have concrete statistical evidence to back up your assessment.

In addition to restricting yourself to actual, factual, verifiable ledger experience, there are a few other things to remember when getting or giving trade credit information:

1. Always record the name, location, and phone number of the company submitting the trade reference.
2. Always ask for and record the full name and title of the person who provided the information.
3. Always ask how current the information in the credit file is.
4. Always ask the credit information source if you are permitted to disclose relevant information to the subject of the credit inquiry—if, and only if—the subject makes such a request.
5. Always record the information exactly as it is given to you. If you are unsure about anything, ask questions.

Other Considerations

To get trade credit information from another creditor, you may be asked to exchange information you have for that held by the trade reference. This could present some ethical problems. Credit granters should not make promises they cannot keep. If you offer to keep the information contained in customer credit files confidential, it should not be disclosed to anybody. For that reason, creditors are cautioned against promising their credit customers absolute confidentiality. Rather, they should protect themselves by including the following on their credit application forms: "The information you provide on this form is confidential. It will be used only for legitimate credit purposes and will be disclosed only in connection with legitimate credit inquiries."

There should be no misunderstanding, however, about the fact that disclosing more than actual, factual, verifiable ledger experience is hazardous. If you say something to a third person that you know is untrue or misleading and it interferes with another person's ability to get credit, you could be in trouble. Remember this point especially when discussing the contents of a credit file with fellow employees, such as salespeople, corporate officials, and office staff. Unless these employees have received proper instruction in the handling of credit information, it is dangerous to provide them with any more information than is absolutely necessary. A small slip of the tongue could result in a gigantic lawsuit.

BANK REFERENCES

Bank references can be an important source of credit information. For such information to be helpful, however, credit granters must know how to interpret the information they get from bankers in response to their inquiries.

The banking community is governed by a strict code of ethics, and banks are cautious when talking about their customers. Bankers rarely say anything negative about their customers. But it is worthwhile to talk to bankers because people often learn more from what isn't said than from what is said. Bankers often use certain code words to describe a customer's handling of his or her account. The credit granter must know how to interpret these words.

Some of the words you are likely to encounter when talking with a banker include:

1. Satisfactory—Accounts described as satisfactory are usually marginal accounts. It is not uncommon for accounts with substantial problems (bounced checks or late loan payments, for example) to be referred to as satisfactory.
2. Good—Accounts described as good are usually average accounts with only a few reported problems.
3. Very Good—Accounts described as very good are usually better than average accounts with no reported problems.
4. Excellent—Accounts described as excellent are usually well-maintained personal or corporate accounts of the bank's most valued customers.

It is important for credit granters to understand what bankers mean when they quote balance ranges. We've all heard the terminology *four-figure account* or *six-figure account,* but what does that mean? And what does it mean when bankers add terms like *low, moderate, medium,* or *high* to their description of a customer's account?

First, a *balance range* is the average amount of money maintained in a customer's account over a specific period of time (normally the preceding thirty days). It is important to know this because creditors must determine whether prospective credit customers have sufficient liquid assets to cover their credit purchases.

There are specific banking terms that apply to the various balance ranges. They are:

1. Nominal—balances from $1 – $99
2. Three figures—balances from $100 – $999
3. Four figures—balances from $1,000 – $9,999
4. Five figures—balances from $10,000 – $99,999

These ranges are pretty broad. For example, there's a world of difference between a four-figure account of $1,000 and a four-figure account of $9,999. For that reason, banks use descriptive terms to narrow the balance ranges. The subclassifications are:

1. Low four figures—$1,000 – $1,999
2. Moderate four figures—$2,000 – $3,999
3. Medium four figures—$4,000 – $6,999
4. High four figures—$7,000 – $9,999

General Rules

For the reasons already stated, banks are very cautious about saying anything that might reflect negatively on their customers. In fact, to get any information at all about a banking customer you are required to follow certain procedures similar to those credit granters observe when contacting trade references.

The three main points are:

1. You must identify yourself and the specific reason for your request.
2. You must guarantee the confidentiality of the information you receive.
3. You should provide specific information about the account you

are inquiring about. If possible, you should supply the proper account name and account number.

While each bank has its own policy regarding the form inquiries should take—telephone or letter—many banks prefer to release bank information only on receipt of a written request. If a written request is necessary, you should write a letter incorporating the three points mentioned above. Because you'll probably write similar letters in the future, it would be wise to design a form letter for this purpose. See figure 4. Your letter should specify the kind of information you're seeking. You'll want to know (1) the date the account was opened, (2) the average balance during the last statement period, and (3) how the account has been handled. It is also important to determine if there are or have been any loans. Thus, you should ask for (1) the beginning loan balances of any loans, (2) the purpose of such loans, (3) whether the loans are secured or unsecured, and (4) whether the loans are being paid as agreed. Finally, you'll want to know if the banker is authorized to release detailed financial information. If the banker has customer permission to disclose such information, your chances of getting it will be improved if you put your request in writing.

If you don't have time to issue a written request for banking information, call the bank and ask the questions you would have asked in a letter. You've got nothing to lose by trying.

Here are a few more things to remember when making bank inquiries. First, if you need fast information from a banker other than your own, contact your own banker first. Your banker will probably be able to avoid some of the red tape and obtain the information you need right away. If you're in good standing with your banker and you keep such requests to a minimum, your banker will probably be happy to help you. Remember Wolner's Rule: *Bankers will do things for other bankers that they may not do for you.*

Check clearing is another area in which contact with your customer's bank may prove useful. Perhaps you have decided to ask your customer for partial or full payment in advance. Maybe you've been getting a lot of bad checks lately. In that case, clear the check by calling the customer's bank. In the case of an unknown customer you'll probably want to do this before delivering any merchandise or performing any services. The following describes how to clear a check:

FIGURE 4
LETTER REQUESTING BANK INFORMATION

DAN A. WOLNER, PUBLISHER   Phone: 612-888-2252

August 23, 19 -

	Subject: ZYX Corporation
	938 Thrifty Road
	Minneapolis, MN 00000

Third National Bank
5870 Deposit Street
Rich, MN 00000

Gentlemen/Ladies:

Your assistance is needed in connection with the extension of credit to the subject noted. The information you provide will be used for business purposes only and will be held in the strictest confidence.

Purpose of our inquiry   *Our experience has been*
Initial order of $_____   Account opened_____ High Credit_____
Credit limit revision___   Owing_____ Past due_____
Change in payment experience___   Last sale_____ Collateral___ Guarantees___
Other_____

    Our file contains: Current trade information___
                                    Financial statement___Date_____

The following information is being requested from your bank. A postage-paid business reply envelope is enclosed for your convenience:

Depository accounts for subject noted:
Account numbers_____
Date(s) opened_____
Average balance(s)_____
Experience and comments_____
_____

Loans: Please list loan number(s), date loan(s) opened, high credit, type of loan(s), amount(s) currently due, amount(s) past due, collateral, personal guarantees (use other side if necessary).
_____
_____

Experience and comments_____

Your name_____Signature_____Date_____

Thank you,

Dan A. Wolner

P.O. Box 39657, Edina, MN 55439-0657

1. Ask to speak to the bookkeeping department of the bank shown on the face of the check.
2. Provide your name and the name of your company. State that you would like to know if there is enough money in the account of one of the bank's customers to cover a check you are holding.
3. Give the bookkeeping department the account number (the coded numbers near the bottom of the check), the name in which the account is listed, the check number, and the amount of the check.
4. If there is not enough money in the customer's account to cover the check, you could be in trouble. On the other hand, there may be a recent deposit that has not yet been credited to the customer's account. In either case, it would be wise to immediately contact the customer for an explanation.
5. If the bank indicates that there is enough money in the customer's account to cover the check, you should be encouraged but not overconfident. The check would be good if you presented it at this very moment. It may or may not be good if you present it this afternoon or tomorrow.

If the transaction involves a lot of money and you doubt the customer's credibility, you may want to take or send the check directly to the customer's bank and present it as a collection item. See figure 5. The bank would then draw funds from the customer's account and present you with a cashier's check drawn on the bank's operating account.

It is important to include an offer of help with every inquiry, written or verbal. Bankers will be more willing to help you if you're willing to reciprocate.

CIVIC, CREDIT, AND TRADE ASSOCIATIONS

There are many organizations that bring business people together to discuss common goals, needs, and concerns. Many credit granters are aware of the advantages of maintaining memberships in civic, credit, and trade associations. Establishing contacts with other credit granters is especially important when it comes to gathering credit information. The following example will illustrate why.

John sells office equipment in a large metropolitan area. His receivables have been growing at a much higher rate than normal. At a recent trade association meeting, John talked with other office

FIGURE 5
LETTER PRESENTING CHECK TO BANK AS COLLECTION ITEM

DAN A. WOLNER, PUBLISHER   Phone: 612-888-2252

September 1, 19 -

Third National Bank
5780 Deposit Street
Rich, MN 00000
ATTN: COLLECTION DEPARTMENT

RE: Submission of attached check as a "Collection Item"

Enclosed is a check drawn on your bank by ZYX Corporation, Check # 999, $539.21, Account #99-999-9. The check was returned to our company marked "Non-Sufficient Funds."

Please process this check as a "Collection Item." Funds sufficient to cover the amount of the check, minus a nominal handling fee, should be mailed to my attention at the following address:

>   Dan A. Wolner, Publisher
>   P.O. Box 39657
>   Minneapolis, MN 55439-0657

If sufficient funds to cover the check are not available within 15 (fifteen) days from receipt of this letter, please return the check to me. A postage paid envelope is enclosed for your convenience.

Please contact me if you have any questions.

Thank you,

Dan A. Wolner

Enclosures

equipment suppliers about his problem receivables. To his surprise, John discovered that nearly all of his competitors were experiencing similar problems. John is now cooperating with the other office equipment suppliers in his area by discussing mutual problems and exchanging trade credit information. The benefits to John and his competitors are obvious.

In highly competitive industries, delinquent customers often take turns establishing credit with one company, charging up to the credit limit, and then moving onto another supplier when the pressure begins to build. The only effective way to deal with this problem is to talk with other credit granters.

CHAPTER 4
ADDITIONAL SOURCES OF INFORMATION

There are several other credit information sources you should be aware of. The following information sources have limited applicability, however. Much will depend on the amount of time you have to make credit-granting decisions, your resources, and your particular credit and sales philosophy.

PERSONAL INTERVIEWS

Many credit managers have found personal interviews to be an effective way to gather credit information. Face-to-face conversations allow creditors maximum flexibility and spontaneity. Of course, not every company can conduct personal interviews. Creditors and their clients may be separated by many miles, and it takes time to schedule and conduct interviews. Regardless, knowing good interviewing techniques is important. Most of these methods will work effectively for telephone interviews as well as personal interviews.

1. Put the person you are interviewing at ease. Get to know the other person before you begin.
2. Spend most of your time listening and not talking.
3. Maintain eye contact.
4. Take accurate notes of what the applicant says.
5. Record your observations of the applicant's demeanor. If the person seems nervous, tense, or upset, write it down.
6. Use the interview as an opportunity to explain your credit terms to the applicant.
7. Make sure to clarify fuzzy points by restating what was said and asking the other person to confirm your understanding.

The questions you ask should closely follow those listed on your credit application. If in doubt about what you can or cannot ask, refer to the section on credit applications in Part I, chapter three.

CREDIT-REPORTING SERVICES

At some point you may be uncomfortable or dissatisfied with the credit information you have gathered. Perhaps you want independent confirmation of the information the credit applicant has provided. Maybe you don't want your customer to know that you're checking on him or her, which often is the case when credit granters deal with large or well-known companies. If so, you may be interested in contacting a credit-reporting service. Credit-reporting services gather, store, and provide credit reports to credit granters detailing the credit habits of millions of individuals and companies. See figure 6.

In theory, these reports are available only to credit-reporting service subscribers. The fee for access to an individual credit report depends on the amount of information available and the amount of information the credit granter requests. Individual credit-reporting service reports are very expensive. It would not be unusual to pay twenty dollars or more for a single report. In addition, credit-reporting service subscribers are generally asked to buy a prescribed number of reports in advance.

Most subscribers order credit reports by telephone. If there is a report on file, sketchy details are given to the subscriber verbally. The report is then mailed to the subscriber. To speed up the process, most credit-reporting services are now capable of providing subscribers with instant access to credit reports via a telephone and computer link. The cost for this type of service is even more expensive.

At least one large credit-reporting service provides rating books in which each company or individual listed is assigned a creditworthiness rating based on estimated financial strength, credit history, company size (number of employees), and other information supplied by the company being rated.

Most credit-reporting services specialize in either commercial or consumer credit reports. There is always some overlap, however, because many businesses are operated by individuals (sole proprietors).

While credit-reporting service reports do serve a valuable purpose, many credit-reporting service subscribers either use the

FIGURE 6
CREDIT REPORT

Dunstreet & Broadbar Credit Reporting Service, Inc.

Dave's Electrical Supply		Report Date		Summary		
3459 Viking Boulevard		July 27, 19 -		Started	1969	
Minneapolis, Minnesota 00000				Payments	See below	
Tel. (000) 000-0000				Sales	$95,000	
David J. Watson, President				Worth	$25,000	
				Employs	6	
				Condition	Good	
				Trend	Steady	

Payments Reported 5-89	Pay Record	High	Due	Past-Due	Terms	Last sale
	Discounts	20000	10000	-0-	2% N30	1 mo
	Discounts	20000	10000	-0-	1% N30	2 mo
	Prompt	1000	500	-0-	N30	2 mo
	Slow 30 days	5000	250	250	N30	1 mo
	Prompt-Slow	5000	1000	500	N30	2 mo

Payment experiences show how bills were paid in relation to terms granted. Sometimes payment beyond terms indicates disputes over merchandise, service, etc.

Finance — On May 27, 19 -, David Watson admitted collections were much improved over last year. Said that inventory will drop significantly by year end. Expects a modest increase in sales over next year.

Public Filings — On April 3, 19 -, a judgment totaling $4,897 was entered against subject in Hennepin County Court. Involves material subject alleges was never received.

Bank — Account maintained nine years, average balance medium to low five-figure account — Second Nat'l Bank, Minneapolis, Minnesota.

History — David J. Watson, President
Rita M. Watson, Vice President
    Incorporated Jan. 16, 1969. Authorized capital consists of 1,500 shares of common stock, par value $1. Paid in capital totals $10,000. David and Rita Watson own capital stock equally.
    David J. Watson born 10/14/33, married to Rita M. Watson 1960. B.A. degree University of Minnesota 1955. Employed by Colonel Electric Corp. from 1955-69, when he started Dave's Electrical Supply.
    Rita M. Watson born 5/7/36. B.S. degree University of Minnesota, 1958. Employed by Erickson's Accounting Service 1958-62.

Operation — General electrical contractor. 350 local accounts mostly commercial. Terms 2% net 30. Peak season spring-summer. Employees 6, owns own building — needs some repair.

It is not permissible to reproduce this report in any manner.

information improperly or place too much emphasis on it. As a result, credit granters are often lulled into a false sense of security. Credit-reporting services solicit credit information from a variety of sources. Some depend on information supplied by the companies they are investigating. Others focus on actual credit experiences reported by other credit granters. The former is much less reliable than the latter. Why? The following is the disclaimer of a credit-reporting service that relies primarily on information supplied by the companies they are investigating:

> This report furnished pursuant to contract for the exclusive use of the subscriber as one factor to consider in connection with credit, marketing, or other business decisions, contains information compiled from sources which we do not control and whose information, unless otherwise indicated in the report, has not been verified. In furnishing this report, we in no way assume any part of the users risk, do not guarantee the accuracy, completeness, or timeliness of the information provided and shall not be liable for any loss or injury whatever resulting from contingencies beyond its control or from negligence.

After reading such a disclaimer it is easy to see why you shouldn't place much faith in these reports. They may be based wholly or partially on unverified information from unidentified sources.*

Regardless of the source of credit-reporting service information, you should never rely exclusively on data contained in a credit report to make a credit decision. While credit reports and ratings can be useful, there is no substitute for information you have compiled and evaluated yourself.

---

*The June 1985 U.S. Supreme Court decision in the case of Greenmoss Builders, Inc. v. Dun & Bradstreet exemplifies the unreliability of such information. In this case a seventeen-year-old high school student employed by Dun & Bradstreet to gather material from a courthouse incorrectly noted that Greenmoss Builders of Wakefield, Vermont, had filed for bankruptcy. Without verifying the information, Dun & Bradstreet negligently included it in a credit report. As a result, Greenmoss Builders failed to get a bank loan during the peak construction season. Although Dun & Bradstreet issued a correction a few days later, Greenmoss sued under the Vermont libel law and was awarded $350,000 in damages. The case was affirmed by the Vermont high court and subsequently by the U.S. Supreme Court.

FINANCIAL STATEMENTS

Few companies are able to convince credit applicants to provide hard financial data. Regardless, there are a number of things everyone should know about financial statements:*

1. Financial statements indicate past performance. They cannot predict future performance.
2. You must have a series of financial statements to know which direction a company is headed.
3. Financial statements are only useful if you know how the company you're analyzing compares to similar companies.
4. To assure maximum reliability, you should make every effort to obtain audited financial information.
5. To determine a company's current financial condition, it's essential to have access to financial information less than six months old.
6. While it's nice to know if a company is financially healthy, that doesn't necessarily mean you'll get paid on time.

If you are able to obtain a financial statement, you'll need to know how to read it. Then you'll want to know how to analyze it and make a few simple calculations. To understand a financial statement, you must know the following balance sheet terms:

1. Current assets—cash, marketable securities, accounts receivable, inventory. Current assets could be converted into cash within ninety days.
2. Fixed assets—land, buildings, machinery, long-term investments. Noncurrent assets take longer than ninety days to convert into cash.
3. Current liabilities—accounts payable, taxes, short-term bank loans, accruals, the portion of long-term debt that is due within

---

*There are several different types of financial statements. To avoid complicating our discussion of financial statements, however, I am referring to a balance sheet when I use the term financial statement. A balance sheet shows a company's financial condition as of a specific date, usually the end of the company's current accounting year.

the next year. Current liabilities are due during the next twelve months.
4. Long-term liabilities—mortgages, long-term bank debt, certain officer loans. Long-term liabilities are debts that are due in more than twelve months.
5. Net worth—common or preferred stock, capital surplus, earned surplus. Net worth is made up of funds provided by the owners to run the business.

Although financial statement analysis is complicated, one can learn much about companies by examining the relationship between the figures listed on a balance sheet. Let's examine the following key ratios (Use figure 7 to make the calculations below. Then turn to figure 8 to check your answers):

1. Current ratio—current assets divided by current liabilities. This ratio shows the amount of current assets available to pay current obligations. The higher the ratio the better able companies are to meet their current obligations. Because this ratio includes both inventory and receivables, it can be misleading. Inventory is not always salable and receivables are not always collectible.
2. Quick ratio—current assets minus inventory divided by current liabilities. This ratio shows the amount of liquid assets available to pay current liabilities. Again, the higher the ratio the better. If there are more current liabilities than liquid assets, the company will find it difficult to meet its current obligations, which is bad for creditors.
3. Current debt to net worth—current debt divided by net worth. This ratio compares the investment made by the owners of the company to that made on a temporary basis by its creditors. The lower the ratio the better. A large amount of debt in relation to net worth means the company is overextended.
4. Inventory turnover—annual sales divided by inventory. This ratio shows how often the company replaces its inventory. The higher the ratio the better. Companies with a sluggish inventory turnover are more likely to be stuck with unsalable merchandise.
5. Accounts receivable turnover—total receivables divided by sales per day (total sales divided by 365). This ratio indicates the number of days it takes the company to collect its receivables. The less amount of time the better. Of course, the goal of every

FIGURE 7
BALANCE SHEET

HARLAN'S MACHINE SHOP
Balance Sheet Dec. 31, 19–

ASSETS		LIABILITIES	
Cash in bank	$ 20,000	Accounts payable	$ 40,000
Cash on hand	2,700	Notes payable	none
Accounts receivable	59,000	Income taxes	3,500
(60+ days ......5,000)		Other taxes	1,700
Notes receivable	none	Interest	1,500
Merchandise inventory	67,000		
(Pledged ....none)		Accrued expenses	2,300
Total current assets	148,700	Total current liabilities	49,000
		Mortgage land & bldgs	29,000
Land & bldgs	35,000	Chattel mortgages	none
Other fixed assets	17,000	Liens mdse, & equip	none
		Other liabilities	none
Due from others (noncurrent)	none	Total liabilities	78,000
Other assets	none	Net worth	124,200
Total assets	$202,200	Total liabilities & net worth	$202,200

Annual net sales $410,000	Cost of goods sold $300,000	Gross profit $126,000	Operating expense $114,000	Net profit for year before taxes $15,000

FIGURE 8
RATIO CALCULATIONS

CURRENT RATIO
$\dfrac{\text{Current Assets}}{\text{Current Liabilities}} \quad \dfrac{\$148{,}700}{\$49{,}000} \;=\; 3.03$

This ratio shows that for every dollar of current liabilities, Harlan's Machine Shop has $3.03 in current assets. The shop's ultimate liquidity depends on the salability of its inventory and the collectibility of its receivables.

QUICK RATIO
$\dfrac{\text{Current Assets} - \text{Inventory}}{\text{Current Liabilities}} \quad \dfrac{\$81{,}700}{\$49{,}000} \;=\; 1.67$

This ratio shows that for every dollar of current liabilities, Harlan's Machine Shop has $1.67 in relatively liquid current assets. This means that there should be sufficient current assets to meet current obligations. Of course, much still depends on the collectibility of the shop's receivables.

TOTAL DEBT TO NET WORTH RATIO
$\dfrac{\text{Total Debt}}{\text{Net Worth}} \quad \dfrac{\$49{,}000}{\$124{,}200} \;=\; .39$

This ratio shows that the creditors of Harlan's Machine Shop have a 39% stake in the business as opposed to 61% for the shop's ownership. This means that the shop is not overly dependent on creditors' funds to finance its operations.

INVENTORY TURNOVER RATIO

$$\frac{\text{Annual Sales}}{\text{Inventory}} \qquad \frac{\$410,000}{\$\ 67,000} \ = \ 6.12$$

This ratio shows that inventory turns over 6.12 times each year, or about every two months. This figure may be misleading because it is based on a year-end inventory figure that may or may not bear any relation to the inventory the shop normally carries during the year. When compared to the inventory figures at year-end of similar firms, however, this ratio indicates that the shop's inventory is warranted by its sales volume.

ACCOUNTS RECEIVABLE TURNOVER RATIO

$$\frac{\text{Total Receivables}}{\text{Total Sales} \div 365} \ = \ 52.52$$

This ratio shows that on the average it takes Harlan's Machine Shop 52.52 days to collect its receivables. If customers are offered normal 30-day credit terms, it appears that the shop is not collecting its receivables efficiently, or that there are a few large uncollected accounts. This could be an indication of trouble.

company is to collect its receivables within its stated terms. If a company's terms are net thirty days, its accounts receivable turnover ratio should be as close to thirty days as possible.

CHAPTER 5
MAKING A CREDIT-GRANTING DECISION

The preceding chapters have given you a working knowledge of some of the most common sources of credit information. You've also learned that credit granting is not a scientific endeavor. While credit granters need to find out as much as possible about each potential credit customer before extending credit, there is no way to be sure the right decision has been made. Remember Wolner's Rule: *Making a credit decision is a lot like using a road map. You may spot a route on the map that will get you where you want to go, but you never know when you might run into detours, road hazards, and adverse conditions.*

Credit sales are necessary to keep the wheels of commerce turning. Therein lies the reason most companies do extend credit, despite the risks: the expectation of profit outweighs the possibility of loss.

In this chapter we'll examine and seek answers to three important questions about making credit decisions: (1) Who is actually responsible for making credit-granting decisions in your company? (2) How much information about a prospective credit customer is enough? and (3) How do you say "no" to a credit applicant?

WHO MAKES THE DECISION?

The question of who in the company makes the credit-granting decisions is often the toughest question a credit granter must face. In a very small company, the owner will make most of the decisions. But what about a slightly larger company—perhaps a company that has delegated its credit duties to a bookkeeper, office manager, or even a credit manager? Is the person responsible for carrying out the company's credit-granting strategy really the one who decides whether or not to grant credit? Maybe not. Typically, administrators, company officials, salespeople, and others outside the credit department have a lot to say about who gets credit. There is nothing wrong with a variety of people participating in the credit-granting process, but confusion often arises when companies fail to clearly define the duties and responsibilities of such people. Your structure of authority should be discussed by, agreed on, and communicated to all those in your company affected by credit-granting decisions. Written guidelines are advisable.

It is often helpful to start with a statement of purpose covering the people involved in and affected by the credit-granting process. The following are ideas for what should be included in a statement of purpose:

1. Purpose—to expand sales through the judicious extension of credit; provide customers with equal and convenient access to company products and services; generate sufficient cash flow to pay current obligations; and guarantee a fair return on investment.
2. Responsibilities—to identify creditworthy customers; enforce credit policy provisions and collect accounts according to approved terms; and minimize the company's exposure to risk.
3. Administration—to make sure company employees observe all legal and ethical standards governing the handling of credit information and the administration of credit; make sure customers and employees understand the credit policy; and implement the provisions of the credit policy.
4. Customer commitment—to actively control receivables and thus avoid the need to increase prices to compensate for credit losses; react to customer problems and concerns quickly; work with customers who are experiencing temporary financial hardship.

Once you have formalized your objectives, delegate sufficient authority to the people responsible for carrying them out. The following tips will help:

1. Decide exactly who reports to whom and about what.
2. Make sure tasks are assigned to people capable of performing them.
3. Explain exactly what each person is expected to do and how each activity contributes to your overall credit-granting strategy.
4. Provide each person with the proper initial training, continuing education, supervision, and motivation to get the job done.

5. Bring all the people involved in the credit-granting process together on a regular basis to discuss ideas, observations, and concerns.
6. Devise methods to evaluate performance.

INFORMATION NEEDED TO MAKE A DECISION

To what lengths should you go to find a reason to extend credit or not to extend credit? Where do you draw the line and finally say, "Based on what I now know, this credit request ought to be accepted or rejected?" At this point, see Part I, chapter one, and reread the section covering the factors that limit the amount of credit information companies ask for. In point of fact, few companies are in a position to request or get all the information they would like to have. But instead of focusing on the factors that limit the amount of information credit granters obtain, let's concentrate on the process of examining the information they do get and the art of making credit decisions.

How much information is needed to make a credit-granting decision? How much time should be spent analyzing such information? The answers to these questions depend on the dollar amount of each sale, the anticipated profit margin, the level of risk you are being exposed to, the general condition of the economy, and other factors. While financial considerations are important in determining the amount of effort you should put into investigating credit applicants, the following factors are equally important:

1. The apparent credibility of the applicant. Credit managers are known for their keen powers of observation. Credit investigations are often triggered when gut reactions and funny feelings indicate that things aren't right.
2. The stability of the applicant. People who frequently change jobs and residences, those without dependable sources of income, and those without an established record will be scrutinized more carefully than others.
3. The availability of verifiable information. If you seem to be having trouble confirming the information provided by the applicant, you'll want to investigate further.

Each credit granter will have to decide exactly how much information is enough. Remember, however, that you should not conduct a credit investigation to justify a decision you have already made. Your purpose should be to honestly evaluate the information you have accumulated. That means letting the information speak for itself. After you add up all the pluses and minuses, you'll be able to determine whether there is sufficient reason to make the sale.

SAYING "NO"

It's tough to deny credit to someone. Few credit granters relish the thought of asking their customers to pay cash. Fewer still are fond of saying "no" to potential credit customers. Unless you automatically grant credit to everyone, however, credit rejections are inevitable. That being the case, you should know the following:

1. Companies offering credit terms cannot arbitrarily grant credit to one person and withhold it from another. Creditors should have guidelines indicating exactly how they determine whether or not a credit applicant is entitled to credit, and if so, how much credit. Applicants meeting the guidelines are entitled to similar treatment.
2. If you are engaged in consumer credit, the Equal Credit Opportunity Act prohibits the denial of credit to any person on the basis of race, religion, national origin, sex, marital status, age (unless the person's age would affect his or her ability to fulfill obligations, such as an elderly person requesting a long-term mortgage), and whether or not the person is on welfare or receiving some form of public assistance.
3. If you are engaged in consumer credit and you intend to turn down an application for credit or approve substantially less credit than was requested, under the Equal Credit Opportunity Act you are required to provide the applicant with the following within thirty days of the completion of the credit application:
   (a) Notification of the action you intend to take; and
   (b) Notification of the specific reasons you are taking such action or notification of the applicant's right to request specific reasons within thirty days.
4. If you are engaged in either consumer or commercial credit and are called on to disclose the specific reason for your denial of credit or your offer of substantially less credit than was requested, remember that sources of credit information should not be identified unless:

(a) The source is a consumer credit-reporting agency;*
(b) The source is another credit granter that has authorized you to disclose its identity.**

Notwithstanding what has already been said, if you have denied credit to an applicant based on credit information received from another credit granter and the source has not given you permission to disclose its identity, at the applicant's request you are required to provide enough facts to allow the applicant to challenge the accuracy of the information.

Softening the Blow

It takes a lot of time and effort to convince customers to purchase your products or services. It's disheartening to give up a sale after all that. Many companies have discovered how to say "no" without destroying the rapport they have built up with their prospective customers. Here are a few ideas:

1. If you are going to deny credit because the credit applicant has failed to give you enough information or the right kind of information, you may be able to resolve the problem simply by asking the applicant for additional information.
2. If the applicant is unknown to you, lacks credit experience, is a borderline case, or has found it difficult to honor obligations in the past, the following options may help you avoid an outright credit refusal:
   (a) Extend or at least agree to consider extending open account terms on future purchases if the applicant will pay cash in

---

*If the source is a consumer credit reporting agency, you need only say, "Our decision to deny credit is based on information contained in a consumer credit report." You should not disclose the exact nature of the information.

**If the source is another credit granter and a credit applicant asks you to identify the source of certain credit information — and you have permission from the source to do so — disclose only the identity of the source and not the information itself.

advance (C.I.A.) or cash on delivery (C.O.D.) for the initial purchase.*

(b) Make the extension of credit contingent on the applicant providing a personal or corporate guarantee, promissory note, or letter of credit.

(c) Request a substantial amount of cash in advance or cash on delivery (perhaps one third to one half of the sale amount), with the understanding that open account terms will be extended on the balance.

By the process of elimination, we have finally arrived at the critical point. What happens when you decide to say "yes"?

---

*On an initial C.I.A. or C.O.D. order it is preferable to obtain guaranteed funds (cash, money order, cashier's check, certified check, or bank wire transfer, for example). If you accept personal or company checks you should review the check clearing procedures covered in part I, chapter three.

CHAPTER 6
SETTING CREDIT LIMITS

All credit prospects are not created equal. Some are more creditworthy than others. It is important, therefore, for credit granters to decide exactly how much credit each applicant is entitled to. This chapter focuses on setting credit limits, both for new and established customers.

NEW CUSTOMERS

Setting credit limits for new customers isn't easy. It doesn't matter how much information you have gathered or how thorough your credit investigation has been. It's still difficult to gauge the intentions of your customers without direct credit experience. Glowing reports of past payment habits may be reassuring but are entirely meaningless if your customer decides to pay everyone except you on time. Extreme caution must be exercised when extending credit to first-time buyers.

What do credit granters have to know to intelligently set credit limits?

1. How much credit does the customer require?
2. Does the customer have sufficient cash on hand to keep a promise to pay? Is credit simply a convenience for this customer?
3. If the customer does not have sufficient cash on hand, is there reason to believe that it will be available by the time payment is due?
   (a) If you are a commercial credit granter, it is important to know how long it takes customers to collect their receivables. There is no better clue to the length of time you'll have to wait for your money.*

---

*You could find this out either by asking the customer or by keeping abreast of general economic conditions through news reports, government publications, and commercial credit reporting services.

(b) Similarly, consumer credit granters ought to be interested in the dependability of the customer's income.
4. How much credit have other suppliers been willing to extend to the customer, and has the customer been worthy of the suppliers' trust? As discussed earlier, reliance on information provided by other suppliers is risky, especially if you're not sure how those credit granters have arrived at their credit limit decisions. But in the absence of direct credit experience, it is useful to know how much confidence other credit granters have in the customer's willingness and ability to keep promises to pay. Similarly, it is important to determine whether the customer has a history of keeping such promises.

Many companies—especially consumer credit granters—are unwilling to spend a lot of time assigning credit limits. These companies generally allow creditworthy customers access to modest amounts of credit. Higher credit limits are assigned on a case by case basis, if necessary and justified.

Regardless of how you determine credit limits for new customers, your ultimate goal is to work with each customer long enough to determine through observation how much credit you can safely extend. Remember, however, that changing conditions may necessitate credit limit changes.

ESTABLISHED CUSTOMERS

After working with customers for a period of time, credit granters have a clearer idea of what to expect. Credit limits are far more meaningful when you know how much credit the customer needs and expects, how long it normally takes the customer to pay, and the predictability of the customer's buying habits.

With that in mind, let's examine the process of setting credit limits in more detail. First, the amount of credit the customer needs must be in line with the amount of credit you feel the customer is entitled to, based on the credit standards you have established. Second, depending on how the customer has handled obligations in the past, you must be willing to live with the customer's current payment schedule. Otherwise you will either have to curtail the amount of credit allowed or find a way to enforce your terms. Third, to decide how much credit the customer will require at any one time, you'll have to analyze the customer's past credit needs and determine how constant or variable, predictable or unpredictable, they have been.

Here are a few examples. If the customer's credit needs last year were $6,000; individual orders totaled approximately $100; invoices were normally paid within terms (net thirty days); the customer's credit needs are expected to remain relatively constant during the next year; you believe the customer's sales volume will be maintained at the present level during the next year; and the customer's monthly purchases are about the same every month, what should the customer's monthly credit limit be?

The following formula is a good rule of thumb to follow when setting credit limits. Take the total amount of credit needed during the year ($6,000), divide it by the number of months over which the customer's orders will be placed (twelve), multiply it by the number of months you'll have to wait for your money (one month), and add the amount of one order (in this case, $100) to allow for payment and payment processing delays:

$$\$6,000 \div 12 \times 1 + \$100 = \$600$$

Seldom, however, are things this easy. While you may have a fix on the total amount of credit needed during the year, the customer may consistently pay you within sixty days, instead of thirty days; each order may total $500, instead of $100; and customer orders may be seasonal in nature (all ordering is done within a four-month period, for example). Using the same formula we used before a much different credit limit results:

$$\$6,000 \div 4 \times 2 + \$500 = \$3,500$$

The credit limit is much higher in this instance than the last because all ordering is done within a four-month period, the customer takes longer to pay, and the amount of each individual order is much larger.*

---

*This is not to imply that you should give delinquent customers preferential treatment. While it is true that the customer in the second example pays within sixty days (which is beyond terms), it was also specified that the customer is a consistent payer. You'll have to decide whether or not you can live with the customer's payment habits before setting your credit limit.

Consider another situation. What if the customer in the second example, instead of placing all its orders during a four-month period, only places 50 percent of its orders during that four-month period and spreads its other orders out over the rest of the year? Here we must deal with differing credit limits for on- and off-season orders:

$$\text{ON-SEASON}$$
$$\$3{,}000 \div 4 \times 2 + \$500 = \$2{,}000$$

$$\text{OFF-SEASON}$$
$$\$3{,}000 \div 8 \times 2 + \$500 = \$1{,}250$$

The formula we have used in these examples can easily be adapted to setting credit limits for new customers as well. Remember, however, that whether you are extending credit to new or established customers, some information about the customer's financial condition and the customer's past payment record is crucial if your credit limits are to have meaning.

Credit limits are not etched in stone. When it comes to setting them, flexibility is the watchword. If you have a chance to capture a larger share of the customer's business, an upward adjustment of the credit limit may be indicated. On the other hand, if you receive signals that your customer or its industry is headed for trouble, you may want to pull back a bit.

CHAPTER 7
MAKING THE STRATEGY WORK

It's no accident that much of this book has been devoted to credit granting and the factors that affect credit-granting strategies. Extending credit is a complicated process. This chapter will fill in the gaps and tie up the loose ends of the discussion.

INFORMATION MANAGEMENT

Much has been said about information gathering, but little has been said about information management. Unfortunately, there isn't enough space here to do justice to the subject. Regardless, there are many information management hints sprinkled throughout this book. You now know that simply asking for credit information isn't enough. You've got to accurately record it. You've got to protect its confidentiality. You've got to guard it from destruction and misuse. You've got to make it accessible. And you've got to update and reevaluate it from time to time. Many credit granters waste the information they gather by failing to observe these rules. The result is a costly duplication of effort that few companies, especially small, struggling companies, can afford.

AN UNTAPPED SOURCE OF CREDIT INFORMATION

A variety of credit information sources have been covered in this book, but there are other sources. The people within your organization are an obvious but often overlooked source of such information. Quite often outside field people, salespeople, and others who maintain contact with your customers have access to a wealth of information. For instance, you may be having trouble verifying credit references, or you're suspicious of the references you have been given. Additional, unbiased trade references may be as near to you as your salesperson is to your prospective customer. During an ordinary sales call it's amazing how much an observant salesperson can learn about a company. Asking office personnel about the company and how it's doing, touring warehouse facilities and noting the names of key suppliers on shipping cartons, chatting with company officials and purchasing agents about sales and profitability trends—these and other methods may provide you with a treasure trove of credit information.

MOTIVATION

Many business people regard motivation as the key to effective credit granting. The topic of motivation is so crucial to credit extending that it warrants a book of its own. Credit granting can be a nerve-racking process, especially for nonprofessional credit managers. Some credit people are virtually incapacitated by their fears, tensions, and anxieties. To be effective, credit people and their supervisors must learn to conquer their fears. Peak performance requires more than ability and a sense of purpose. You've got to have the determination to meet challenges head-on.

The following formula illustrates my point:

$$\text{Capability} + \text{Purpose} \times \text{Determination} = \text{Results}$$

A results attitude doesn't just happen, however. It is the by-product of enlightened management—constructive criticism, praise, understanding, and support. By developing confidence in their ability to react to difficult problems, people with receivable-control responsibilities will be able to concentrate on the primary goal of credit management—helping people obtain and retain credit. In that light, credit people will soon discover that their job is not to solve problems. Rather, it is to suggest solutions and create an atmosphere that makes it possible for others to solve their own problems. Frustration decreases when credit and collection people realize it's not their responsibility to impose solutions on others. Self-satisfaction increases when attention is focused on the problem-solving process, not on the problems themselves. Motivation increases when people feel good about what they're doing and why they're doing it. By motivating others, people become motivated themselves. And motivated people get results.

TRAINING

Training is another topic that deserves more space than we are able to give. People are the secret to any credit-granting strategy.

Proper training is the only way to assure effective implementation of that strategy. Regardless of your company's size, the level of experience of your credit and collection staff, or your sales volume, a regular program of in-house training is a must. Beating the odds means keeping your people informed and up-to-date.

It doesn't matter whether the training is conducted by company personnel or outside experts. You may ask your staff to educate themselves by reading books; you could arrange periodic staff meetings to discuss recurring problems and potential solutions; you might encourage attendance at credit seminars; or you might do a combination of all three. Why take the time or spend the money for training? Training pays for itself, and increased effectiveness means fewer losses and larger profits. Besides, training is inexpensive. One legal problem, slip of the tongue, or silly mistake could easily cause trouble, so the adage, "An ounce of prevention is worth a pound of cure," is certainly appropriate for credit granting.

COMMUNICATION

Communication is the key to winning the cooperation of others. By making sure your fellow employees and customers understand your procedures and policies, you'll greatly reduce losses. But communication also means listening, and even if you listen carefully, it's easy to get the wrong impression. So you must verify what you thought you heard by restating. This is especially important when explaining your credit terms to a customer, checking credit information, and giving instructions to credit and collection personnel.

It is very important to do a good job at the credit-granting stage. Remember Wolner's Rule: *The success of your credit-granting strategy will depend on the amount of effort you expend.*

PART II. COLLECTING ACCOUNTS ACCORDING TO APPROVED TERMS

Part II of this book underscores the fact that credit sales really aren't sales until the money has been collected. To collect as much money as possible, credit granters must be constantly on the lookout for collection problems. When potential problems are spotted, decisive action must be taken to prevent them. Remember Wolner's Rule: *A buck in the bank is worth two on the books.*

It seems, however, that many companies are reluctant to confront their delinquent customers. Some are afraid of triggering a customer backlash that could hurt business. Others are simply uncomfortable about discussing collection problems with their customers. Still others regard collection efforts as a waste of time because they assume that no matter what they do their customers will pay when they're ready to pay.

Considering the misconceptions that seem to surround the debt collection process, it's easy to understand why many people in the business community have problems with credit control. In some circles, debt collecting is considered to be a sleazy endeavor, and debt collectors are believed to be abusive, callous, and gruff. In truth, however, successful debt collectors are an honorable lot. They are patient, understanding, inquisitive, and persistent. They boost business by detecting and resolving problems that might otherwise damage customer relations. They also search for ways to help financially distressed customers meet their obligations.

Many creditors, however, sit idly by while their hard-earned profits are eaten up by the mounting costs of slow-pay and no-pay customers. Ashamed and reluctant to admit they don't have all the answers, these misguided entrepreneurs pin their hopes entirely on the good intentions of their customers, instead of actively promoting credit responsibility. During credit and collection lectures and seminars, I often present case histories of actual collection problems. There is no better way to illustrate. Remember Wolner's Rule: *If you ignore simple, manageable problems long enough, they will become complicated and unmanageable.* As in other areas of business management, inaction is the biggest enemy of the credit granter. Many people simply surrender to collection problems out of frustration, while others equivocate and procrastinate.

Part II begins by asking the question, "Why don't people pay their bills on time?" Some of the reasons are so obvious creditors tend to overlook them. Others are so unexpected creditors seldom think of them. Successive chapters cover the importance of collection follow-up and the effects of past-due receivables on profitability. These chapters were designed to help credit granters answer the question, "Can I afford to implement a really effective receivable control system?" The last two chapters of Part II are devoted to collection letter writing and telephone collection calling. Based on more than a decade of research and practical application, these chapters thoroughly cover the two most widely used debt collection methods.

Without a doubt, knowing how to collect money is critically important to the overall success of your receivable-control strategy. Remember, however, that an effective response to credit and collection problems depends as much on an intelligent approach to credit granting and the timely use of alternative collection measures as it does on collection expertise.

CHAPTER 8
WHY PEOPLE DON'T PAY ON TIME

There are many different reasons why people aren't able to pay their bills promptly or choose not to pay promptly. Miscommunication between buyer and seller over credit terms is one of the leading reasons for delinquency. By taking a few simple precautions, however, credit granters could all but eliminate this problem. Credit granters must provide their customers with written explanations of their credit terms and conditions at the time of sale. They should also take the time to discuss the terms with the buyer to make sure he or she understands them.

For example, each fall I do a series of credit and collection seminars in Minneapolis. To promote the seminars, I mail brochures to selected clients and prospects. Last year, on the basis of competitive bids, I selected a new print shop to produce my brochures. My order totalled nearly $1,000. The print shop manager took my order without saying anything to me about the shop's credit terms. He simply told me the brochures would be ready in about a week. No signs were posted in the shop, nor was I provided with a written explanation of the shop's payment policy. The manager didn't ask for any credit references, and he showed no interest in determining how I was going to pay for the brochures. I wasn't even asked to sign the order. Exactly one week later I went back to pick up my brochures. When I inquired about the shop's credit terms, the manager told me, "All orders are C.O.D." Rather incredulously I asked again, this time offering to provide whatever credit information he needed. His response was, "I'm sorry, sir. We don't extend credit to first-time buyers." With obvious disgust, I wrote a check for my order. I wondered, though, what the shop manager would have done if I had been unable to pay him, or if I had refused to pay him. As it turned out, I didn't have to wonder very long.

While waiting for my brochures to be loaded into the car, another first-time buyer walked up to the counter and announced that he, too, was there to pick up an order. Predictably, the shop manager told him, "All orders are C.O.D." After making a frantic effort to find some money and coming up empty, the customer turned to the shop manager and admitted he couldn't pay for the order. Then the customer said, "I've got to have these circulars for a meeting tomorrow morning. If you can't give them to me now, you might just as well keep them and forget the whole thing." After pondering his predicament for a moment, the shop manager let the customer take the order without paying. So much for the shop's C.O.D. policy!

By failing to make the shop's payment policy clear to his customers and by not determining whether customers were capable of paying for their purchases on delivery, the print shop manager was taking a big chance. After all, there was little he could do if a customer either could not or would not pay on delivery, except: (1) deliver the merchandise without being paid and risk not being paid at all, or (2) withhold delivery of unsalable merchandise. Neither choice would be very appealing.

To correct this situation the print shop manager should:

1. Obtain enough information to determine if the customer is able to pay for purchases on delivery, explain the shop's C.O.D. policy to his customers, and allow customers who are able to pay on delivery to do so. Obtain cash in advance or a substantial deposit (twenty-five to fifty percent) from all other customers.
2. Obtain enough information to determine if the customer is eligible for credit, explain the shop's credit policy to eligible customers, and extend credit. Obtain cash in advance or a substantial deposit (twenty-five to fifty percent) from all other customers.
3. Obtain cash in advance.

Remember that if you intend to enforce your credit policy, you've got to make sure your customers understand it. And to make sure your customers understand it, you've got to take the time to explain it to them when you take the order.

Personal problems and unforeseen circumstances are two more common reasons why people don't pay their bills on time. It's not surprising that experiences like death, divorce, serious injury, and unemployment are disruptive to people. When day-to-day problems place legitimate obstacles in the way of prompt payment, credit granters must be patient and understanding. Unmercifully hounding customers who are doing their best to meet their obligations will only make a bad situation worse. Credit granters do have a right to ask (1) the reason why the customer is unable to pay, (2) an explanation of how the customer intends to meet his or her obligations, and (3) an assurance of customer cooperation. More often than not, past-due customers respond positively to those who offer encouragement and support during a crisis.

Money mismanagement is another reason people don't pay their bills on time. Some people find it extremely difficult to manage their money. No matter how much money they make, they're perpetually in debt because they knowingly spend more than they take in. Wary credit granters are usually able to spot such people during their credit investigations. If, however, you're not fortunate enough to identify them and deny or severely restrict the amount of credit you extend, you'll have to work hard to recover your money. A casual collection approach will only give the poor money manager additional time to get deeper into debt.

Some people don't pay their bills on time even though they have plenty of money. These people play an intentional waiting game, stalling until the credit granter makes a serious move to collect what's due. They do so because they know a delay in paying their debts will make it possible to put their money to better use. Why should they pay you on time if you'll let them use your money for an extra thirty, sixty, or ninety days? Many companies find it difficult to handle customers who are able to pay on time but don't. Fearing the loss of business that might result from pressuring these people, many creditors simply give them additional time to pay. But a "wait and see" attitude on your part will give these customers the advantage because their real purpose is to buy time. It's not smart to give additional time to people who are capable of paying. You have a right to your money on the day it is due. That's when you must ask for it—no matter who the customer is.

Finally, some people don't pay, won't pay, and never intended to pay. These people are out to take whatever they can get at your expense. Fortunately, only a small percentage of credit customers engage in illegal, deceptive, or fraudulent activities. Nevertheless, credit granters must be vigilant to weed out these undesirables.

CHAPTER 9
COLLECTION FOLLOW-UP

Because people don't always pay on time, it is essential to have a system of collection follow-up to motivate credit customers to meet their obligations. Used properly, your follow-up system will help you spot potential problems and react appropriately.

Collection follow-up should begin as soon as the account becomes past-due. Many creditors make the mistake of providing their customers with an automatic grace period beyond the actual due date. While you should take into consideration the amount of time it takes to process payments and update your accounts receivable ledger, collection follow-up should begin as soon after the due date as possible. You should not condition your customers to expect more time to pay than was originally agreed on.

SPOTTING POTENTIAL PROBLEMS

Small business owners and managers have many responsibilities. They're expected to perform all their regular duties, manage a variety of day-to-day crises, and control their receivables. Sometimes it isn't easy to keep everything straight, especially when it comes to staying on top of delinquent accounts. Starting from the premise that problem receivables aren't likely to jump up and bite you, you must do the following things to keep yourself informed and up-to-date about your credit customers:

1. Make contact with delinquent customers as soon as possible after their accounts have become past-due. This will enable you to identify and react to potentially serious problems before they get out of hand. It may even help you avoid some problems altogether. Reacting swiftly to delinquent accounts means having access to current payment information. Payments must be posted promptly and collection personnel notified quickly.

Few things are more discouraging for collectors than contacting customers for payment and finding out they have already paid.
2. Record pertinent information about your credit customers. The more information you have about your customers the better. It's especially important to note promises and commitments. That will help you determine which customers are trustworthy and which are not.
3. Follow-up when you said you would. It's important to make it clear to your customers that you expect them to do what they have agreed to do, when they have agreed to do it.
4. Remain in regular contact with past-due customers until their accounts have been paid, settled, or written off. Tenacious and persistent creditors are less likely to fall prey to unscrupulous customers.

DEVELOPING A FOLLOW-UP SYSTEM

The type of follow-up system you use will depend on the size and sophistication of your company. Regardless of the system you use, however, the purpose is the same: to differentiate between your paying and nonpaying customers and to collect your money as soon as possible.

Most credit granters use one of following systems:

1. A manual ledger system, where notations are written right into the ledger as payments are posted and receivables are evaluated;
2. A card system, where file cards are made up for each past-due customer and arranged in chronological order depending on when payment is due and follow-up is needed;
3. An aged-receivables system, where each month invoices are classified by the number of days they are past-due: 0 – 30 days, 30 – 60 days, 60 – 90 days, 90 days and over;
4. A duplicate invoice system, where duplicate copies of past-due invoices are pulled and placed in files for action appropriate to the number of days each invoice is past-due.

TIMING

It is absolutely critical for companies to follow up on time. This point cannot be overemphasized. But what does "following up on time" mean? For example, if your terms are net thirty days, when should your follow-up begin? Many credit granters automatically wait ten, twenty, or thirty days or more beyond their stated terms before making contact with delinquent customers. That's not smart. Customers will soon learn that they've got an additional ten, twenty, thirty or more days to pay. When they do, they'll take advantage of it.

Credit granters must let their customers know that they consider prompt payment to be important from the start. That means asking for your money when it's due. There are special circumstances, however, in which a brief delay beyond the due date would be acceptable. For example, many companies have customers forward their payments to bank "lockboxes." This system allows customers to forward their payments directly to your bank. The bank processes and deposits customer payments into your operating account. Photocopies of the checks and payment application information is then sent by mail or messenger to you for posting. While payments are immediately deposited in your operating account, there is no way for you to know about them until you receive the pertinent information from the bank. All of this takes time—time for the bank to process the payments, time to send the remittance information to you, and time for you to post the payments to the appropriate accounts. If your bank is located nearby, the delay may be only a day or two. If your bank is far away, it may take considerably longer. If you use the lockbox system, it is advisable to put off your collection efforts long enough to determine whether payments have been received. If you don't wait until you have the facts, you won't be able to verify whether customers who claim to have paid have done so or not. That will mean getting back to customers who haven't paid and incurring the wrath of those who have.

EASING INTO THE COLLECTION PROCESS

Most companies use a low-key approach on accounts that have just crossed the line between current and past-due. Collection efforts at this point have two main purposes: (1) gently reminding the customer of his or her obligation, and (2) attempting to discover if a problem exists. A brief informational letter, free of any heavy demands, is usually the best approach. See figure 9. A reminder of this sort should reacquaint the customer with your terms and reaffirm your willingness to continue serving the customer conscientiously and diligently in return for payment as agreed.

FIGURE 9
REMINDER LETTER

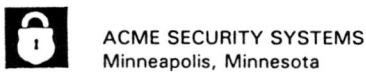

ACME SECURITY SYSTEMS
Minneapolis, Minnesota

March 14, 19 -

Mr. Jim Sawyer
JIM'S GEMS
1915 Golden Highway
Miner, Minnesota   00000

Mr. Sawyer:

Customers say they appreciate reminders when their payments are due. That's why I'm writing to you now.

If you haven't already done so, please mail your check for $195.00 to reach us by March 24, 19 -.

Thank you,

ACME SECURITY SYSTEMS

Lorinda B. Jensen
Lorinda B. Jensen
Customer Service

Not surprisingly, perhaps, some companies view reminders—sent shortly after the due date—as costly, unnecessary, and offensive to the customer. While some customers may complain (some will complain no matter what you do), most will understand and respect your concern. More important, you'll notice a dramatic improvement in your cash flow.

What happens if your first reminder is unsuccessful? How long should you wait before contacting the customer again? The key word in debt collecting is continuity. Credit granters should make contact—either by sending additional notices or placing telephone calls—each week until the customer pays or responds. You should use increasingly stronger collection measures on unresponsive customers until a satisfactory payment arrangement is reached, a professional debt collector is called in, or the account is written off.

HANDLING RESPONSES TO INITIAL INQUIRIES

Customer responses to initial collection inquiries are fairly predictable. The following are the most common responses, along with a few suggestions on how to handle them:

1. If your customer responds by sending payment in full, you should say "thank you." On a good day you might even say "thank you very much!"
2. If your customer responds by promising to send payment in full by a certain date that is acceptable to you, it's wise to acknowledge the promise in writing. Remember to cite the specific terms of the agreement.
3. If your customer responds by giving you:
    (a) An explanation—Immediately contact the customer by telephone or letter. It is important to be understanding. Remember, however, that your main purpose is to obtain a specific payment commitment.
    (b) A complaint about your merchandise or services—Take the necessary steps to verify and rectify the situation. If that involves contacting the customer by telephone or letter, or communicating with others in your organization to obtain more information, do it. A determination of the validity of the complaint should be made as quickly as possible. If you are at fault, you should resolve the problem and send the customer a written apology. If an adjustment is necessary,

issue it. Then make sure to ask for prompt payment of the adjusted amount. If the customer's complaint is not valid, write to the customer at once and explain your position. Then request immediate payment of the amount due.

   (c) An excuse that is intended to buy time or avoid a payment commitment—Immediately contact the customer by telephone or letter. Focus your attention on bringing the customer's account up-to-date no matter how persistent the customer is in dodging the issue.

4. If your customer responds by denying responsibility for the debt, you should take the necessary steps to verify the customer's identity and the validity of the debt. If you have contacted the wrong party or your billing is incorrect, a written apology should be issued and corrective action taken. If you determine that you have contacted the proper party and your billing is correct, you should provide documentation and press for full, immediate payment.
5. If your customer responds by not responding at all, you must be prepared to intensify your collection efforts. See Part II, chapters eleven and twelve.

Remember that customer responses to initial collection inquiries should always be handled quickly, efficiently, courteously, and professionally. Most customers will appreciate your diligence and respond positively. Those trying to fool you will soon discover that they can't buy additional time from you or deter you from doing your job.

CHAPTER 10
THE IMPACT OF PAST-DUE RECEIVABLES

It now seems appropriate to underscore the importance of collection effectiveness by studying the impact of past-due receivables on profitability. Small, undercapitalized companies should pay particular attention to this information.

There are two statistical measurements that have a lot to say about business conditions and prospects: (1) profit margins, and (2) interest rates.

1. Profit margins—Simply stated making a profit is hard work. One key profitability indicator is the relationship of aftertax corporate profit to corporate domestic income. This ratio tells us how much profit corporations end up with out of what they bring in as income. Graph 1 shows the 20-year trend for this indicator. You don't have to be a financial wizard to understand why it is more important than ever for companies to control their receivables. During periods of shrinking profitability, uncollected receivables make it that much more difficult for small businesses to compete.

2. Interest rates—The cost of borrowing money is another factor that makes it difficult for companies to stay in business. Small businesses are especially susceptible to fluctuations in interest rates. Graph 2 shows the 20-year trend for this indicator. Simply put, companies cannot afford to have needed operating capital tied up in delinquent receivables. By keeping receivables current, companies will reduce their need to borrow money and thus reduce interest expense.

GRAPH 1
RATIO OF AFTERTAX CORPORATE DOMESTIC PROFITS TO CORPORATE DOMESTIC INCOME

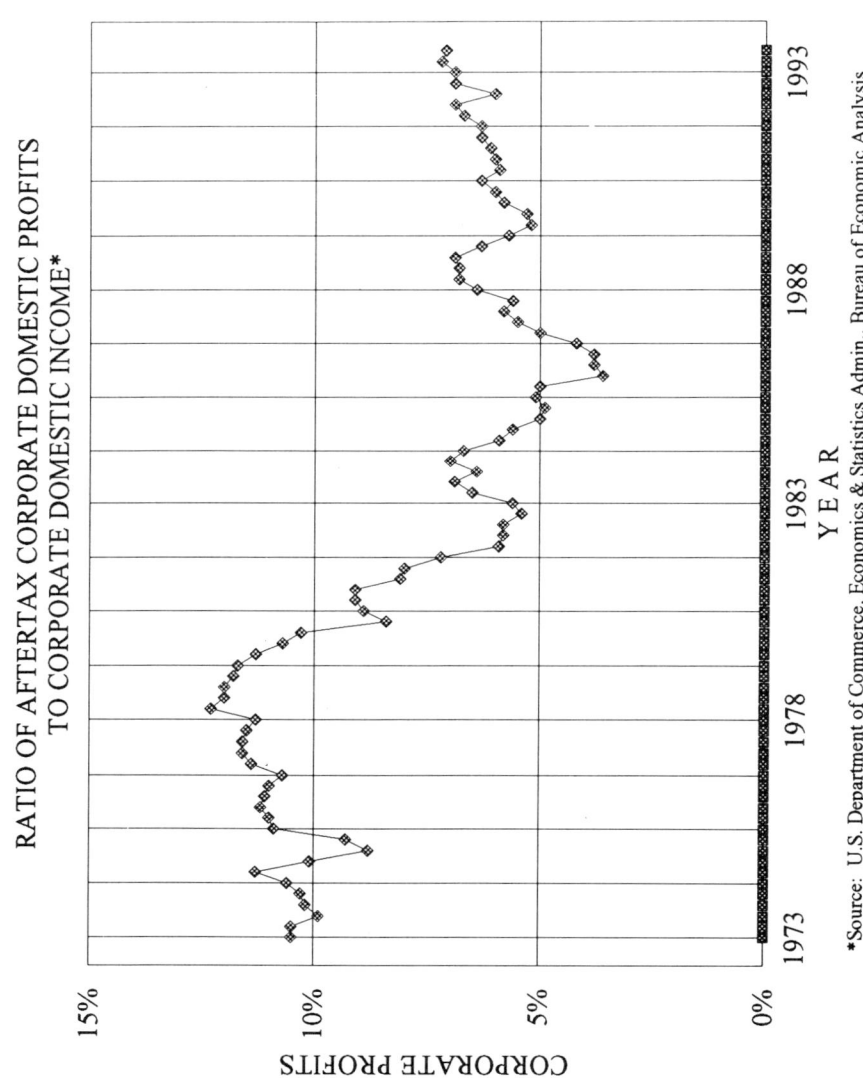

*Source: U.S. Department of Commerce, Economics & Statistics Admin., Bureau of Economic Analysis

GRAPH 2
BANK RATES ON SHORT-TERM BUSINESS LOANS

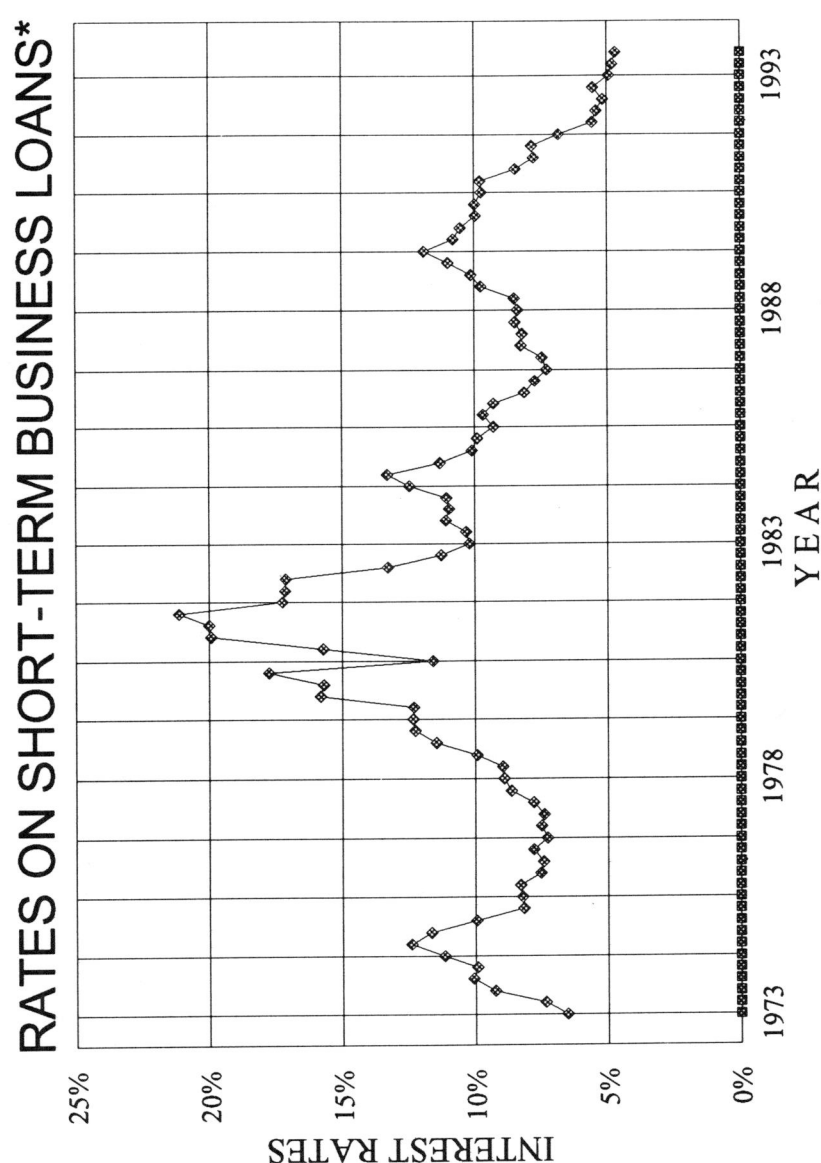

*Source: U.S. Department of Commerce, Economics & Statistics Admin., Bureau of Economic Analysis

TABLE 1
ADDITIONAL SALES DOLLARS NEEDED TO OVERCOME BAD-DEBT LOSSES

DOLLAR AMOUNT OF BAD-DEBT LOSS

	$500	$1,000	$1,500	$2,000	$2,500	$5,000
2.00%	$25,000	$50,000	$75,000	$100,000	$125,000	$250,000
4.00%	$12,500	$25,000	$37,500	$50,000	$62,500	$125,000
6.00%	$8,333	$16,667	$25,000	$33,333	$41,667	$83,333
8.00%	$6,250	$12,500	$18,750	$25,000	$31,250	$62,500
10.00%	$5,000	$10,000	$15,000	$20,000	$25,000	$50,000
12.00%	$4,167	$8,333	$12,500	$16,667	$20,833	$41,667
14.00%	$3,571	$7,143	$10,714	$14,286	$17,857	$35,714
16.00%	$3,125	$6,250	$9,375	$12,500	$15,625	$31,250
18.00%	$2,778	$5,556	$8,333	$11,111	$13,889	$27,778
20.00%	$2,500	$5,000	$7,500	$10,000	$12,500	$25,000

*Note: All amounts rounded

TABLE 2
NET PROFIT IN DOLLARS ON A GIVEN SALE
AT A GIVEN PROFIT MARGIN

DOLLAR AMOUNT OF SALE

	$1,000	$2,500	$5,000	$7,500	$10,000	$12,500
2.00%	$20	$50	$100	$150	$200	$250
4.00%	$40	$100	$200	$300	$400	$500
6.00%	$60	$150	$300	$450	$600	$750
8.00%	$80	$200	$400	$600	$800	$1,000
10.00%	$100	$250	$500	$750	$1,000	$1,250
12.00%	$120	$300	$600	$900	$1,200	$1,500
14.00%	$140	$350	$700	$1,050	$1,400	$1,750
16.00%	$160	$400	$800	$1,200	$1,600	$2,000
18.00%	$180	$450	$900	$1,350	$1,800	$2,250
20.00%	$200	$500	$1,000	$1,500	$2,000	$2,500

*Note: All amounts rounded

The following example will help explain these points. Assume that you wait 4 months beyond your normal terms before collecting a total of $5,000 owed to you by several past-due customers. Further assume your unwillingness or inability to collect this money leaves you short of working capital and forces you to borrow $5,000 for a period of 4 months to cover the shortage. If we assume a 6 percent aftertax profit, we know that your gross profit on a $5,000 sale will be $300. See table 2. If we also assume an 8 percent interest rate on a 4-month short term business loan, we know that the loan's interest will be $133. After subtracting the loan interest from your $300 gross profit, you'll end up with a profit on a $5,000 sale of just $167. By failing to collect your money when it was due, and instead having to borrow the necessary working capital, your profit margin on a $5,000 sale has been reduced from 6 percent to 3.3 percent.*

Several other factors should also be considered. Small businesses with "aging" receivables on the books will find their borrowing power severely limited. Bankers providing accounts receivable financing may not be willing to lend money at any price to businesses carrying past due receivables. In addition, by failing to collect money when it is due, you lose the opportunity to use that money to pay outstanding bills, or purchase needed products and services. Inadequate cash flow is one of the major causes of business failure.

Inflation is another reason why companies should keep their receivables current. Regardless of current conditions, inflation is always lurking in the background. And, even at modest rates, inflation means that receivables will always be worth less when they are collected than when they were originally due.

---

*Regardless of future trends in profits and interest rates, borrowing to finance receivables will always be a losing proposition. Razor thin profit margins dictate the timely collection of receivables to avoid unnecessary interest expense.

76 Turning Debts into Dollars

Using the same example mentioned earlier and presuming an annual inflation rate of 3.6 percent, a 4-month delay in collecting $5,000 means the money you eventually collect will be worth $60 less than it would have had you collected it on time. Subtracting this loss, as well as the $133 loan interest from your aftertax profit of $300, you will end up with a measly profit of just $107 on a $5,000 sale. That's a net profit of 2.1 percent.

In addition to what has already been said about the effects of past-due receivables on companies, there is an even more compelling reason for keeping your receivables current: receivables become less collectible with age. Unfortunately, many companies have learned this vital lesson the hard way. Some have even been forced out of business because they failed to take the necessary steps to keep their accounts current. Diligent credit granters do see their share of slow-pay and no-pay accounts, too, but they have learned how important it is to resolve delinquent accounts quickly. Inaction only gives past-due customers more time to sink deeper into debt, leave town, or close their doors.

Many companies are understandably concerned about the cost of implementing an effective collection follow-up system. They ought to be more concerned about the cost of not implementing such a system, however. An ineffective collection strategy will probably result in your having to (1) place more accounts with professional debt collectors (see Part III, chapter fifteen), or (2) write more accounts off as bad debts. The following examples explain:

1. If you place a $5,000 non-legal, commercial account with a collection agency, and the agency is successful in collecting the entire amount, the usual fee would be about 25 percent ($1,250). Assuming a 6 percent profit on the original sale ($300), you would have lost $950, and you would need to generate approximately $16,000 in additional sales just to break even. See table 1.
2. If you place a $5,000 legal, consumer (retail) account with a collection agency, and the agency is successful in collecting the entire amount, the usual fee would be about 50 percent ($2,500). Assuming a 6 percent profit on the original sale

($300), you would have lost $2,200, and you would need to generate approximately $37,000 in additional sales just to break even.
3. If neither you, nor an agency are successful in recovering any of the $5,000, and you end up taking the entire $5,000 as a bad debt loss, what then? Assuming a 6 percent profit margin, you would need to generate approximately $83,000 in additional sales just to break even.

Thus, it's not hard to see why it's dangerous to turn your back on your receivables. To minimize risk and collection expense, credit granters must move quickly to bring past-due customers up-to-date, obtain specific payment commitments, and resist the temptation to wait just a little longer before taking action. Remember Wolner's Rule: *Time doesn't collect money—people do.*

CHAPTER 11
WRITING EFFECTIVE
COLLECTION LETTERS

Most credit granters build their collection systems around a series of collection letters, even though collection experts generally agree that telephone calls are more effective than letters in collecting money. What's the reason for this apparent contradiction? Collection letters are more practical than telephone collection calls. Because most companies use prewritten form letters, it's relatively quick and easy to contact hundreds, perhaps thousands, of delinquent customers in the time it would take to make only a handful of telephone collection calls. Collection letters also provide credit granters with tangible proof of their efforts to make contact with past-due customers. This could be important if it becomes necessary to call in a third-party debt collector or take legal action to recover your money. In addition, collection letters are usually preferred for contacting customers who have only been past-due a short time. The proverbial "friendly reminder" is believed to be less threatening to customers than a telephone collection call during the period shortly after the scheduled due date.

EIGHT CARDINAL RULES

Many books of this type provide credit granters with prewritten form letters. This book, however, will teach you how to effectively write your own collection letters. It also will show you how to identify and correct weaknesses in the letters you're presently using. It takes time and a lot of practice to write effective letters, but the time you spend learning to do so will pay off in the future.

There are eight basic rules that must be observed when writing any kind of letter:

1. Keep it short and simple. This rule is known as the "K.I.S.S. Principle." Remember Wolner's Rule: *Brief, well-written letters*

are always more effective than long letters. The purpose of a letter—any letter—is to motivate the reader to act. Long letters (those over one page in length) usually turn readers off, and it's hard to motivate someone who is turned off.

2. Avoid the use of cumbersome words and phrases. Some people fill their letters with complicated words to impress others.* While a good vocabulary is something to be proud of, it is best to stick to small, easy to understand words and phrases when writing letters. For example:

Awkward	**Preferred**
You'll find your June statement attached to this communication.	Attached is your June statement.
With reference to the attached copy of our last letter, we would sincerely appreciate a prompt response.	Your prompt reply to the attached letter would be appreciated.

3. Keep your sentences and paragraphs short. We have already explained the importance of controlling the length of your letters and the length of individual words. You should also control the length of your sentences and paragraphs. Split up long and complicated sentences instead of joining them together with conjunctions like *and* or *but*. If you don't you'll put the reader to sleep. Also avoid rambling paragraphs. Paragraphs needn't be longer than a few short sentences.
4. Carefully organize the information you put in your letters. Move logically from one thought to another.
5. Focus on the word *you*. Many people overuse words like I, me, my, we, and our. By overloading your letters with first-person pronouns, you may make the reader feel inferior or unimportant. When composing your letters focus your attention

---

*Word usage is critically important to the overall readability of letters. Appendix A contains information for improving the readability of your letters.

on the reader. As you gain letter writing experience, you'll learn how to use the word *you* to shift the emphasis away from yourself and towards the reader. For example:

Instead of	**Say**
I need to know the reason why your account is past-due and I need to know now!	If you have a reason for paying late, you should tell us about it now.
It seems to me that I have given you more than enough time to explain why your account is still unpaid.	You've had plenty of time to explain why your account hasn't been paid.

6. Check your writing for repetition. Letters can be shortened by eliminating redundant words and phrases. For example:

Redundant	**Preferred**
During the month of June your account was past-due.	Your account was past-due in June.
Please mail your payment to our office, which is located in the city of Minneapolis.	Please mail your payment to our Minneapolis office.

7. Be as specific as possible. Say what you have to say clearly and concisely. If you hide your message between the lines, the reader may ignore it, misunderstand it, or miss it altogether.
8. Accentuate the positive. Make a serious effort to begin and end all letters on a positive note. An upbeat opening is especially important when conveying bad news. Those receiving your letters will be more receptive to what you have to say if you

begin with positive thoughts instead of negative thoughts. For example:

Poor	**Preferred**
Unfortunately we cannot ship your July order until payment is received for your June invoice.	Your July order will be shipped just as soon as your June invoice is paid.
You'll be in a lot of trouble if you don't call us by June 5th.	You can do yourself a favor by calling us by June 5th.

FIVE ESSENTIAL ELEMENTS OF A COLLECTION LETTER

The next step in learning how to write effective collection letters is learning the five essential elements of a collection letter: (1) the identifier, (2) the grabber, (3) the clarifier, (4) the motivator, and (5) the concluder.

The Identifier

The identifier identifies the person or persons to whom you are directing your letter. It consists of the inside address (which includes the first and last name of the person you are writing to; the company name, if you are writing to a company; the street address; city; state; and zip code) and a separate recognition line. The recognition line consists of a courtesy title, such as Mr., Ms., Mrs., and the last name of the person to whom your letter is addressed. It replaces the archaic salutation, or greeting, that customarily follows the inside address in business letters. The use of a salutation in a collection letter is inappropriate.* For years I started all my letters with the standard salutation "Dear Mr. Cunningham." I

---

*I believe the salutation, the complimentary close, and certain other letter writing conventions have outlived their usefulness in general business correspondence as well.

thought there was no harm in opening a business letter by writing "Dear Mrs. Cunningham" because nobody really pays any attention to the word "dear" anyway. Then one day I asked myself, "If nobody pays any attention to the word 'dear,' why am I using it?" I haven't used it since. That decision raised the question of how a business letter should begin. I ruled out using only the first name of the person I was writing because collection letters shouldn't sound chummy. I finally decided to simply begin my letters with "Mr. Cunningham" or "Ms. Cunningham." I call this the recognition line because its purpose is to call special attention to the name of the person you are writing.

The Grabber

The grabber gets the reader's attention and intices him or her to read on. When writing collection letters, it is important to give the reader a reason to keep reading. Some credit granters use humor in their letters to grab the reader. But past-due accounts are no laughing matter, and it is unwise to give delinquent customers the impression that owing you money is something to chuckle about.

You should also know the following about the grabber:

1. It should be placed at the beginning of your letter.
2. It should be short, usually one or two sentences.
3. It should focus attention on the reader.
4. It should arouse the reader's curiosity—without deceit or sensationalism.
5. It should be encouraging, not threatening or accusatory.

The following examples will help you think of your own effective grabbers. For a mild collection letter:

"Talk to us. We're here to help you."

For a demand letter:

"Isn't this the opportunity you've been waiting for?"

For a final demand letter:

"There's still time. Shouldn't you make the most of it?"

The Clarifier

The clarifier explains (1) why you have written, and (2) what you expect the reader to do. The clarifier should be the following:

1. Factual—Avoid useless speculation about why the customer hasn't paid you. Concentrate instead on what you do know. You may wish to reacquaint the customer with your credit terms. You should recap your previous collection efforts and the results achieved. You must specify the amount of money due and the exact date you expect the customer's account to be paid up.
2. Frank—Make sure the customer understands the message you are trying to convey. Explain why you're concerned about the customer's failure to pay as agreed. Then propose a plan to bring the customer's account up-to-date.
3. Firm—State your position confidently and positively. Make it clear that you anticipate the customer's cooperation. When requesting payment, remember a tentative request is likely to lead to a tentative response. Avoid phrasing payment requests in the form of a question like "Will you clear up your account by June 30, 19 -?" Instead, say, "We'll expect you to clear up your account by June 30, 19 -."
4. Fair—Appeal to the customer's sense of fair play. This can often be accomplished by describing the considerable lengths you have gone to in attempting to resolve the customer's account. Fairness also means providing the past-due customers with a face-saving "escape hatch." It makes good sense to give the customer an opportunity to avoid drastic collection measures by contacting you or paying you. Shoving the past-due customer into a corner is likely to trigger a defensive reaction that will only make your job more difficult. For example, for a mild collection letter:

"Your account is now past due. If this is just an oversight, I trust you'll mail your check for $250 to reach us by June 15, 19 -."

For a demand letter:

"Despite the fact that your account is sixty days past-due, you have a chance to bring your account up-to-date right now with no questions asked. Just make out a check for $500 and mail it to reach us by June 15, 19 -."

For a final demand letter:

"Your failure to respond to our letters and phone calls has given us no choice but to explore the use of more drastic collection measures. You do, however, have one last opportunity to clear your account and avoid such action. Remember, this is your final notice. Your check for $1,000 should be mailed to reach us no later than June 15, 19 -."

The Motivator

The motivator is designed to convince the customer that it makes sense to cooperate with you. It also stimulates the customer to do what you have requested. The essence of credit management is being patient and perceptive enough to discover what motivates each delinquent customer. That means looking at each collection problem from the customer's standpoint and using an approach that appeals to the customer's self-interest.

What self-interest appeal should you use? That depends on what and how much you know about the past-due customer:

1. If the customer has consistently paid on time until now, you may wish to emphasize the importance of preserving a good credit rating or maintaining a high credit limit.
2. If the customer pays promptly most of the time but occasionally takes too long to pay, you may wish to emphasize the benefits of retaining credit privileges or continuing to buy from your company.
3. If the customer seldom if ever pays on time, you may wish to emphasize the inconvenience of doing business on a C.O.D. or C.I.A. basis or enduring legal or collection agency action. For example, for a mild collection letter: "You've worked hard to achieve a fine credit reputation. We'd like to help you preserve it." For a demand letter: "Prompt payment will help ensure uninterrupted delivery of your future orders." For a final demand letter: "By paying us now, you'll be spared the unpleasantness of having to deal with the XYZ Collection Agency in Minneapolis, Minnesota."

The Concluder

The concluder signals an appropriate end to your remarks. The concluder includes a "closer line," a signature line, and possibly a postscript. The "closer line" replaces the archaic complimentary close that has customarily been used to end business letters. For reasons stated earlier in this chapter, I believe the complimentary close has outlived its usefulness. A collection letter ending with "sincerely," "sincerely yours," or "yours truly" seems absurd to me. The closer line could be dropped altogether without diminishing the effectiveness of your collection letters. If you are compelled to use a closer line, I recommend a simple "thank you."

The signature line encompasses a series of lines at the end of a business letter. Together these lines identify the writer of the letter. A complete signature line includes the name of the company the writer represents, the writer's full name, signature, and information to help the reader locate and communicate with the writer. For example:

DAN A. WOLNER, PUBLISHER

(Leave 3 or 4 blank spaces for signature)

Dan A. Wolner

It is important for collection letters to be signed. Signatures give letters a human touch that unsigned computer notices lack. People respond better to people than they do to computers. The more you're able to convince your customer that you have personally written and signed all your letters, the better. It's advisable to actually sign your letters, instead of using a stamped or preprinted signature. It's also best to sign your name in colored ink (red, green, blue, and brown are good) to give your letters a distinctive flair, which will make them more noticeable. On the line beneath your signature, type your full name. It's important for delinquent customers to be able to picture you in their mind's eye. If you leave off your first name and use only initials it's harder for the customer to identify with you.* On the line beneath your typed name, specify your department, telephone number, extension or mail station to make it easier for customers to respond to you.

Many credit granters like to tack postscripts onto their collection letters. Postscripts are a great way to give the customer additional motivation. Legible, handwritten postscripts in colored ink (preferably red) are especially effective. You'll further heighten the effect of your postscripts by placing them conspicuously either at the extreme bottom or top of your letters.

PRACTICAL APPLICATIONS

One of the best ways to gain practical collection letter writing experience (other than actually writing collection letters) is to analyze letters others have written. Later you should examine the collection letters you're currently using to determine if improvements are necessary.

The collection letters shown in figures 10 through 14 are marked "before" and "after." The "before" letters are composites of letters actually written and used by credit granters. The "after" letters represent my revisions of the "before" letters, based on the information presented in this chapter.

---

*Many companies disguise the identities of their collectors by replacing their first names with initials. I've been told that this is often done to prevent anyone from determining whether a letter has been sent by a male or female collector. Since the effectiveness of a collector is a function of training and experience, not gender, I advise collectors to use their full names on all letters.

FIGURE 10
COLLECTION LETTERS

 STATEWIDE TELEPHONE, INC.
Minneapolis, Minnesota

February 4, 19 -

Ms. Eva Lou Shoemaker
1915 Mankato Street
Glenn Valley, Minnesota 00000

```
BEFORE
```

Dear Ms. Shoemaker:

Is there some problem?

I'm sorry to have to remind you that your account is now overdue. I assume you simply overlooked our invoice #1111, dated January 4, 19 -, in the amount of $257.00.

I hope you'll send a check as soon as possible to bring your account up-to-date.

Thank you,

STATEWIDE TELEPHONE, INC.
Collection Department

STATEWIDE TELEPHONE, INC.
Minneapolis, Minnesota

February 4, 19 -

Ms. Eva Lou Shoemaker | AFTER |
1915 Mankato Street
Glenn Valley, Minnesota   00000

Ms. Shoemaker:

Have you noticed?

According to our records, Invoice #1111, dated January 4, 19 -, $257.00, is now overdue.

In order to bring your account up-to-date, we would appreciate your mailing a check in the amount of $257.00, to reach us by February 14, 19 -.

Thank you,

STATEWIDE TELEPHONE, INC.

Bill L. Kelley
Bill L. Kelley
Collection Department

FIGURE 11
COLLECTION LETTERS

 DATA CONTROL, INC.
Minneapolis, Minnesota

April 15, 19 -

Mr. Mike Nelson
SOFTWARE SUPPLY COMPANY
8402 Dual Drive
Silicon City, Minnesota 00000

BEFORE

Mr. Nelson:

Why haven't you contacted us?

This is the second time I have been forced to write to you about past-due invoice #3333, dated March 2, 19 -, in the amount of $956.30. Do you need a copy of this invoice?

Unless you have a pretty good excuse for not paying within our net 30-day terms, I'm going to have to ask you to issue a check in the amount of $956.30, by April 25, 19 -.

Sincerely yours,

DATA CONTROL, INC.

M. A. Monahan
M. A. Monahan
Credit Manager, Ext. 422

DATA CONTROL, INC.
Minneapolis, Minnesota

April 15, 19 -

Mr. Mike Nelson
SOFTWARE SUPPLY COMPANY
8402 Dual Drive
Silicon City, Minnesota   00000

AFTER

Mr. Nelson:

Perhaps you need a copy?

Enclosed is a copy of invoice #3333, dated March 2, 19 -, in the amount of $956.30. This is the past-due invoice I wrote to you about on April 2, 19 -.

Since our terms are net 30 days, it is important that you mail your check in the amount of $956.30, to reach me by April 25, 19 -.

Thank you,

DATA CONTROL, INC.

Mary A. Monahan
Mary A. Monahan
Credit Manager, Ext. 422

Enclosure

FIGURE 12
COLLECTION LETTERS

MINNESOTA HOME STORE
Minneapolis, Minnesota

June 24, 19 -

Ms. Lera G. Miller
1234 Sauk Rapids Street
Elcor, Minnesota 00000

BEFORE

Lera:

Don't you think this has gone far enough?

It disappoints me that you apparently take the advantages of credit with our firm so lightly. Despite two or three letters requesting payment of seriously past-due invoice #5555, dated April 24, 19 -, in the amount of $515.00, you still have not bothered to respond.

At this point, it doesn't look like you have any hope of preserving open-account credit with us, and it's obvious that we'll probably have to use more intensive collection efforts to collect the money due us. Why don't you just give us a break and send us your check in the amount of $515.00?

Thank you,

MINNESOTA HOME STORE

Andy F. Hopkins

Andy F. Hopkins

MINNESOTA HOME STORE
Minneapolis, Minnesota

June 24, 19 -

Ms. Lera G. Miller
1234 Sauk Rapids Street
Elcor, Minnesota 00000

```
┌─────────────┐
│   AFTER     │
│─────────────│
└─────────────┘
```

Ms. Miller:

Remember how important you felt it was to establish credit with our firm?

Because I know you appreciate the advantages of open-account billing privileges -- convenience, quick order processing, extra time to pay -- it concerns me that two previous requests for payment of seriously past-due invoice #5555, dated April 24, 19 -, in the amount of $515.00, have gone unanswered.

To preserve the benefits of open-account credit, and avoid more intensive collection efforts, it is urgent that you mail your check in the amount of $515.00, to reach me by July 3, 19 -.

Thank you,

MINNESOTA HOME STORE

Andy F. Hopkins

Andy F. Hopkins
Furnishings, Mail Station 3

FIGURE 13
COLLECTION LETTERS

CLEAN TOWEL SUPPLY COMPANY
Minneapolis, Minnesota

September 10, 19 -

Mr. Jeff Ventura
BODYBUILDERS, INC.
538 Bushwacker Avenue
Turnbuckle, Minnesota 00000

BEFORE

Mr. Ventura:

We are at our wits end.

We have tried everything to get you to pay your seriously past-due balance on invoice #7777, dated June 10, 19 -, in the amount of $1,524.90, but you have chosen not to reciprocate. Now it's time for your to pay up, or else.

I'm going to see to it that our lawyer goes after you for illegally trying to cheat us out of our money. You'll be sorry, unless you mail your check in the amount of $1,524.90, to reach me by September 20, 19 -.

Thank you,

CLEAN TOWEL SUPPLY COMPANY

Roberta S. Blackburn
Roberta S. Blackburn

CLEAN TOWEL SUPPLY COMPANY
Minneapolis, Minnesota

September 10, 19 -

Mr. Jeff Ventura
BODYBUILDERS, INC.
536 Bushwacker Avenue
Turnbuckle, Minnesota   00000

```
           AFTER
    _____
```

Mr. Ventura:

<u>FINAL NOTICE</u>

Patience has its limits.

Despite our persistent efforts to motivate you to pay invoice #7777, dated June 10, 19 -, in the amount of $1,524.90, you have failed to do so. I now have no alternative but to request full and immediate payment.

To avoid referral of your account to the law firm of Dewey, Cheatum and Howe, Minneapolis, Minnesota, your check in the amount of $1,524.90 should be mailed to reach me no later than September 20, 19 -.

Thank you,

CLEAN TOWEL SUPPLY

Roberta S. Blackburn
Roberta S. Blackburn
Credit Department, Ext. 155

FIGURE 14
COLLECTION LETTER SERIES

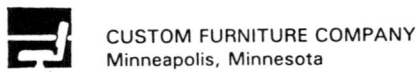

CUSTOM FURNITURE COMPANY
Minneapolis, Minnesota

Ms. Sally Raider
7904 Al Davis Avenue
Stabler, Minnesota 00000

BEFORE

RE: Invoice #9999, September 3, 19 -, $750.00

Ms. Raider:

COMMITMENT LETTER
October 14, 19 -

Thank you in advance for your prompt attention to this matter.

Recently you proposed a plan that would clear up your account. You told me that you would mail one check in about two weeks, and another about two weeks after that.

I'm afraid I cannot guarantee that we won't be forced to use more intensive collection efforts to collect this money, if you fail to make your payments as agreed.

BROKEN COMMITMENT LETTER
October 29, 19 -

We don't trust you anymore.

When we gave you credit, we figured you would pay our bills on time. When you didn't, I demanded payment. You reluctantly agreed to a plan that would bring your account up-to-date. Then, right off the bat you miss your first payment.

Frankly, I'm fed up with your lies. If you don't pay within a week or so, I'm going to place your account with a collection agency.

CUSTOM FURNITURE COMPANY

Edward P. Hammer
Edward P. Hammer
Collection Manager

CUSTOM FURNITURE COMPANY
Minneapolis, Minnesota

Ms. Sally Raider
7904 Al Davis Avenue
Stabler, Minnesota 00000

AFTER
_____

RE: Invoice #9999, September 3, 19 -, $750.00

Ms. Raider:

COMMITMENT LETTER
October 14, 19 -

Your cooperation is appreciated.

During our telephone conversation October 13, 19 -, you agreed to bring your account up-to-date. You have promised to mail your first check in the amount of $375.00 to reach me by October 28, 19 -, followed by a second check of $375.00 to reach me by November 12, 19 -.

By making your payments as agreed, more intensive collection efforts will be avoided.

BROKEN COMMITMENT LETTER
October 29, 19 -

Relationships are built on trust.

When credit was extended to your company, we trusted that you would pay our bills on time. When your payment was late, I called, and you promised to bring your account up-to-date by mailing one check for $375.00 to reach me by October 28, 19 -, and another check for $375.00 to reach me by November 12, 19 -. Now that commitment has fallen through.

Frankly, trust has its limits. To avoid placement of your account with the XYZ Collection Agency, Minneapolis, Minnesota, your check in the amount of $750.00, should be mailed to reach me no later than November 12, 19 -.

CUSTOM FURNITURE COMPANY

Edward P. Hammer

Edward P. Hammer
Collection Manager

Analysis of the "Before" and "After" Collection Letters

Figure 10

1. The word "Dear" is unnecessary.
2. Avoid overuse of words like "I, me, my, we, and our."
3. Don't open by suggesting there might be a problem.
4. Don't apologize for requesting payment.
5. Confidently state what you want the customer to do.
6. Be specific about the amount of money and the date you expect payment.
7. Always include your full name, signature and location information (department, telephone number, extension, or mail station).

Figure 11

1. Don't open with a personal attack on the customer.
2. Always say, "Enclosed is," never say "Please find enclosed."
3. Provide the customer with a copy of the invoice instead of giving him/her excuse to delay payment by requesting it later.
4. Don't solicit excuses from the customer for not paying.
5. Close with "Thank you," instead of "Sincerely yours, yours truly," etc.
6. Always specify that checks are to be "mailed" not "issued."

Figure 12

1. Never refer to the customer by his/her first name (Replace "Lera," with "Ms. Miller.")
2. Appeal to the customer's sense of responsibility.
3. Express confidence (not pessimism) about the likelihood of the customer doing what you ask.
4. Spell out some of the advantages of open-account credit with your firm.
5. Always offer the customer an "escape hatch."
6. Specify exactly when you expect payment to arrive.
7. Make it easy for the customer to locate you by providing your department, telephone number, extension or mail station.

Figure 13

1. Avoid the appearance of desperation.
2. Appeal to the customer's sense of fairness.
3. Explain exactly what you expect the customer to do.
4. Never make idle threats like "Pay up or else."
5. Specify the name and location of the attorney or law firm you intend to use.
6. Never accuse the customer of dishonesty or illegal conduct.
7. Don't engage in personal attacks.
8. Avoid overuse of words like "I, me, my, we, and our."

Figure 14

Commitment Letter

1. Avoid the use of archaic words and phrases like "Thank you in advance for your prompt attention to this matter."
2. Be specific about the date the commitment was obtained.
3. Spell out the details of the commitment (exact amounts and specific dates when payment expected).
4. Stress the word "promise" when referring to the commitment.
5. Focus on the benefits of the customer honoring the plan, not the drawbacks of failing to honor it.

Broken Commitment Letter
1. Appeal to the customer's sense of responsibility.
2. Remind the customer that you have taken all reasonable steps to resolve the situation.
3. Remind the customer what was promised.
4. Never accuse the customer of lying.
5. Specify the name and location of the collection agency you intend to use.
6. Always ask the customer for a specific amount (payment in full) by a specific date.

STAYING OUT OF TROUBLE

Use caution when writing collection letters. There are a number of important things credit granters must never do:

1. Never threaten actions you do not intend to take. For example, if you threaten to refer the customer's account to a collection agency or collection attorney if the customer fails to pay by a certain date, you should do so within a reasonable period of time.
2. Never accuse the customer of illegal conduct. Only a court of law is able to determine whether or not a customer has acted legally.
3. Never communicate defamatory statements to third parties. If you include derogatory information about your customer in a letter (to your customer or to a third person) you should have proof to back up your assertions. If you knowingly communicate false information about a customer to a third person, or through your negligence you allow false information to fall into the hands of a third party, you could be sued for libel.
4. Never use fraud or misrepresentation to collect debts. It is illegal to attempt to scare customers into paying by sending letters that give the impression that they have come from the courts, government agencies, attorneys, or collection agencies when they have not.

CHAPTER 12
TELEPHONE COLLECTION STRATEGIES

The telephone is a marvelous collection tool. Yet there is more to collecting over the telephone than just picking up the receiver and demanding payment. The success of your telephone collection strategy depends largely on your ability to master specific telephone collection techniques. It's just as important, however, to know when to use the telephone to collect money and when to collect by letter.

When would it be advantageous to collect by telephone?

1. When time is a factor—It's faster to make a telephone collection call than it is to send a collection letter.
2. When you need immediate feedback—Direct and immediate interaction between creditors and their customers is possible during a telephone collection call. By using the telephone, parties who may be miles apart have an opportunity to discuss and resolve problems on the spot, without the delays associated with collecting by letter.
3. When your letters have been ignored—You're more likely to get through to a reluctant customer by telephone than you are by letter. Many past-due customers ignore their mail, but few can resist answering their telephone. Of course, delinquent customers have been known to dodge telephone calls, too. But if you're successful in reaching someone at the customer's place of business or residence (even if it's not the person you really need to talk with), you may have an opportunity to slip a carefully worded message through to the proper party. You also may be able to gather enough information to facilitate contact with the proper person later on.*

---

*It is not advisable to discuss specific collection problems with people at the customer's place of business or residence who lack sufficient authority

4. When the customer's sincerity is in doubt—Collectors can learn much more by conversing with delinquent customers on the telephone than they can by exchanging letters. It's important to hear how people say things. A person's tone of voice is often indicative of his or her willingness to cooperate. For example, a collector would have good reason to interpret the statement, "I'll pay you next week," quite differently, depending on whether the words were said with sarcasm, anger, humor, or contrition.

THE FIVE PHASES OF A COLLECTION CALL

Collection calls generally consist of five distinct phases: (1) preparation, (2) identification, (3) fact-finding, (4) agreement, and (5) follow-up.

Precall Preparation

There are certain things you must do before picking up the telephone to make a collection call. Some people refer to precall preparation as "doing your homework," "precall investigating," or "preplanning." It doesn't matter what you call it as long as you do it.

Precall preparation is necessary for three reasons. First, knowledgeable collectors are prepared collectors. Second, prepared collectors are self-confident collectors. Third, self-confident collectors are effective collectors.

Validating the Amount Due

Before attempting to collect a debt by telephone or letter, credit granters must be certain the debt in question is, in fact, due. The following questions prove helpful in validating debts:

1. Has the customer already paid us? Be sure that all payments made by the customer have been posted. It's also a good idea to check other accounts with similar names and account numbers for possible payment misapplications.

---

to solve such problems. Instead, simply leave your name and your company's name; obtain the names of the individuals who are authorized to answer your questions; determine when these individuals will be available to speak with you; and say only that you are calling about a serious business or personal matter.

2. Did the customer receive our invoice? If you're certain the invoice in question was mailed, you should verify that it was mailed to the correct address and routed to the right person.
3. Does the customer have a legitimate reason to withhold payment? This question will trigger other questions. For example:
   (a) Have we created or contributed to this problem? Don't overlook the obvious (merchandise shipped to the wrong location, damaged merchandise, and billing errors, for example).
   (b) Are we or should we be aware of a problem? Check with others in your company (especially shipping, sales, service, credit, and collection personnel) to determine whether there are any unresolved customer complaints.
   (c) If we are aware of a problem, has action been taken to solve it? If the customer is awaiting some action on your part before sending payment, make sure appropriate action has been taken. For example, if the customer needs a corrected invoice, send it. If the customer needs a backordered part, ship it. If the customer needs an explanation of some sort, supply it.

Evaluating the Customer's Payment Record

Next, a careful review of the customer's payment record should be conducted. Customers usually fall into one of the following categories:

1. When-due payers—Customers who generally pay when they're supposed to pay. Since these people are self-motivated, collection action is rarely necessary.
2. When-asked payers—Customers who generally pay when they're asked to pay. Motivating these folks to pay is usually a matter of sending a few collection notices or making an occasional telephone collection call.
3. When-ready payers—Customers who generally pay when they feel like paying. These are the tough ones. You'll probably have to pull out all the stops to motivate these customers to pay.

Customer payment records tell credit granters much about the general character and reliability of their customers. They may even provide clues to the most effective collection method to use.

Analyzing the Customer's Collection File

While payment records contain a wealth of information about customer habits and tendencies, your collection files will prove even more useful to you in figuring out how to collect your money. Properly documented collection files are valuable because they describe:

1. The extent to which your previous efforts have been successful. By knowing what has and hasn't worked in the past, you'll have a better idea of what will work in the future. For example, if you're contacting a customer who ignores your collection letters but responds promptly to your collection calls, you'll be able to make the necessary adjustments in your collection strategy.
2. The customer's past excuses for late payment. Some customers rely on the same excuses for late payment time after time. By identifying compulsive excuse-givers, you'll be in a better position to overcome their excuses. That's not to say you'll never be fooled by a creative excuse. Fortunately, most of the excuses aren't very creative. "The check is in the mail" is still a favorite excuse, as is "We're having cash flow problems." "The check is in the computer and we can't get it out" is now gaining popularity.
3. The extent to which your response to delinquent accounts is predictable. Some credit granters get into ruts. For instance, they may start out every month by calling customers at the beginning of the alphabet. By doing that they send a subtle message to delinquent customers at the end of the alphabet that they can safely wait a few extra days or perhaps weeks before paying. Why not start at the end of the alphabet one month, the middle the next month, and the beginning the month after that? Then reverse the order. Better yet, pick the past-due customers you're going to call at random. It's best to keep your customers guessing.
4. The details of your previous collection attempts. It's essential to know the names of the people you have contacted, where you have contacted them, when you have contacted them, and what you accomplished by contacting them. Specific information of this kind will prove invaluable in the future. For example, when contacting past-due companies you'll run across two kinds of people: (1) those who are willing and able to help you resolve delinquent accounts, and (2) those who aren't. If it becomes

necessary to contact the same company again, you'll want to know how to reestablish contact with people in the first group and how to avoid those in the second.

Mapping Out a Plan of Action

After validating the amount due, evaluating the customer's payment record, and analyzing the customer's collection file, map out your collection strategy by pulling together everything you have learned about the customer. Before you pick up the telephone to place a collection call, it's important to have a contingency plan in mind to resolve the problem. Since new facts may come to light during your telephone conversation with the customer, your plan should be flexible enough to allow for a bit of last-minute fine tuning. For example, the job of every collector is to press for prompt payment of the full amount due. If you discover that the customer is not in a position to immediately bring his or her account up-to-date, you should be ready to propose a payment plan.

To succeed as a telephone collector you must be fully acquainted with the facts of each case and the habits of each customer. After completing your precall preparation, you'll be ready to intelligently discuss collection problems with past-due customers, overcome their objections, and resolve their accounts.

Identification of the Parties

The second major element of a successful telephone collection call is the process of identifying yourself and the person you're speaking with. The importance of the identification process cannot be overemphasized. In Part I you learned that the credit-granting stage is the best time to ask a customer for the names of people to contact in the event of collection problems. If you've got the names of specific people to speak with, now is the time to use them. If you don't, now is the time to get them.

Confirming the Identity of the Other Person

The first step in the identification process is making sure you've got the right person on the other end of the line. Discussing collection problems with innocent third parties is dangerous. If you spread false or misleading information about a customer to a third party you could be sued for slander. In addition, speaking with the wrong person is a waste of the collector's time. Most collectors are far too busy to spend their valuable time talking with people who can't help them.

The easiest and safest way to confirm the identity of the person you are speaking with is to ask the question, "Is this Mr. Anderson with the ABC Company?" If the answer is, "yes," it's safe to continue. If you are dealing with a company and you don't have the name of a specific person to speak with, you should ask to speak with the person who pays the bills. Try to get the person's name before you're connected. When you are connected, confirm the person's identity by asking the question, "Is this Mr. Anderson with the ABC Company?" If the answer is, "yes," it's safe to continue. If you aren't able to come up with the name of a specific individual, simply ask, "Is this the person who pays the bills for the ABC Company?" If the answer is, "yes," get the person's full name before continuing. If the people at the customer's place of business you have previously spoken with have not been helpful, you should ask to speak with the controller, treasurer, or president. Again, try to get the person's name before you're connected with him or her. When you are connected, ask, "Is this Mrs. Anderson with the ABC Company?" If the answer is, "yes," it's safe to continue.

When addressing a delinquent customer, always put a "Mr.," "Ms.," or "Mrs." in front of the person's name. While there's nothing wrong with also adding the person's first name ("Is this Ms. Mary Anderson with the ABC Company?"), collection experts generally agree it's not a good idea to converse with past-due customers on a first name only basis.

Identifying Yourself

To properly identify yourself, you should immediately provide the person on the other end of the line with three pieces of information: (1) your name, (2) your company's name, and (3) the purpose of your call. If I were placing a collection call, I would say: "This is Mr. Wolner with Business Credit Concepts. I'm calling about the $500 past-due account the ABC Company has with our firm." Remember that collectors should avoid the use of their first names. Opening your conversation with the more formal "Mr. Wolner" reinforces the seriousness of the situation.

After properly identifying yourself, stop talking for a few moments. The reason for this pause will be explained below.

Fact-Finding

Fact-finding is the third major element of telephone collection calling. No matter how much you learn during the precall preparation, you won't know all the facts until you speak directly with the customer. But how do you begin a conversation with someone who owes you money? How do you get the customer to open up? Most collection experts agree that a brief pause at the end of the identification process is the most effective way to get the ball rolling.

The Tactical Pause

A period of silence—from two to five seconds—at the end of the identification process sends a signal to the customer that it is his or her turn to speak. Most delinquent customers succumb to a nearly irresistible urge to end the silence by saying something. If the customer decides to speak, the collector must listen first and then react. If the customer remains silent, the collector should immediately press for payment in full.

Listening

It is essential for every collector to learn when to talk and when to listen. If you are successful in motivating the customer to talk, don't interrupt. Remember Wolner's Rule: *A good listener is a good collector.* The following will help remind you of the importance of listening:

1. L stands for "Let the customer talk." To find out how and when payment will be made you must let the customer talk. Interrupting and putting words in the customer's mouth will not solve the problem.
2. I stands for "Identify the central problem." Most customers have lots of problems. The collector's job, however, is to listen closely enough to pinpoint the central problem.
3. S stands for "Search out solutions." You'll find it much easier to search out potential solutions if you allow the customer to tell you what's wrong.
4. T stands for "Tune-in the customer." If you're tuned-in to what your past-due customers are saying, you're more likely to be able to help them.
5. E stands for "Earn the customer's respect." Thoroughness and knowledge should accompany careful listening. If you exhibit these qualities, you'll earn the respect and gain the confidence of your delinquent customers.
6. N stands for "Narrow the scope of the problem." By giving delinquent customers a chance to speak, you'll be able to narrow

the scope of collection problems and focus on the most important issues.

Reacting

Customers who choose to speak following the tactical pause normally respond by promising to pay, explaining why payment is late, complaining about goods or services, denying responsibility, or challenging you to collect. The following tips will help you react appropriately no matter which response you receive:

1. Payment promises—All payment promises must be framed in specific terms. If the customer has promised to send payment in full, it is the collector's job to get all the details. How much money will be paid, in what form, when, and to whom? Idle promises to pay as soon as possible are worthless. If the customer proposes a payment plan, see "Negotiating a Payment Plan" later in this chapter. If the customer makes a settlement offer, see Part III, chapter 13.
2. Explanations of late payment—Unless you're able to prove that a customer is lying, you've got no choice but to accept his or her explanation for late payment. Your job is to facilitate the resolution of problems, not to debate the circumstances that led to them. Customer explanations of late payment often involve misunderstanding, carelessness, and procrastination. In such cases it is the collector's responsibility to clear up any doubts the customer may have about his or her responsibility to pay promptly.

    Some customer explanations of late payment involve very serious problems (physical or emotional illness, unemployment, and disaster, for example). Even when confronted with serious obstacles to payment, however, creditors must insist on proof that the problem exists, customer cooperation, and future payment. It's possible that a customer's explanation of late payment could be an excuse to avoid payment.
3. Complaints about goods and services—Complaints about goods and services must be taken seriously. In fact, creditors have an ethical, moral, and (in the case of retail credit granters) legal obligation to document, verify, resolve, or refute customer complaints promptly. Efficient handling of complaints also builds customer confidence and loyalty and allows the creditor to collect what is due. It also lets unscrupulous customers know

that you won't let unfounded complaints stop you from collecting your money.

Don't lose control of the situation by "passing the buck." Collectors must assume total responsibility for resolving the complaints reported to them. That means following up to make sure required action is taken whether that action is to be taken by you or someone else. Remember that you must (1) investigate the complaint, (2) take necessary action, and (3) report your findings to the customer. Only then should you renew your collection efforts.

4. Denials of responsibility—Customers who deny responsibility by claiming that the bill is owed by someone else, the bill has not been received, or the bill has already been paid are entitled to the same protection and courtesy as customers who complain about goods and services. If, after conducting a thorough investigation, you're sure your billing is valid, it is advisable to send the customer proof of delivery (or similar documentation) by certified mail with return receipt requested. Payment of the amount owing should then be sought.

5. Challenges to the creditor's authority—Some customers are willing to admit they owe you money, but instead of paying they challenge you to collect it. This tactic is often used by delinquent customers with small-balance accounts. Defiant customers will try just about anything to distract or upset you. When confronted with defiant customers remember to stay calm. No matter how persistent the customer is in avoiding a payment commitment, the collector must continue to ask for one.

If reasonable efforts to obtain a payment commitment fail, a final demand letter should be sent and the account placed with a third-party debt collector. See Part III, chapters 15 and 16.

Asking for Payment in Full

If the customer is uncommunicative following the tactical pause, the collector must immediately ask for payment in full. There should be no question in the customer's mind that you intend to collect the full amount due and nothing less. Your request for payment in full

1. Must be presented confidently. You should presume an affirmative response.

2. Must be specific as to when payment is expected. You are advised to ask for payment by a particular date.
3. Should identify the desired form of payment and the method of delivery.

For example, if the customer owes you $500, say, "I'm counting on you to drop off your money order for $500 at my office on or before June 30," or "Your check for $500 should be mailed to reach me by June 30."

Don't be negative. Never say, "I don't suppose you'll be able to send us any money right now, will you?" Don't hint that you're willing to accept less than payment in full—even if you are.

The measures taken by the collector following a request for payment in full will depend entirely on the customer's reaction. If the collector is able to obtain a payment commitment from the customer, the agreement must be finalized. If the collector is not able to obtain a payment commitment from the customer, further steps will be necessary to obtain one.

Asking Fact-Finding Questions

It would be great if all past-due customers automatically came to their creditors to explain why they paid late and when they intend to pay. Unfortunately, many delinquent customers are reluctant to do that. It then becomes the collector's responsibility to get the facts by asking carefully worded questions. Collection experts call these questions "fact-finding questions." Good fact-finding questions (1) require past-due customers to supply specific reasons for late payment, and (2) provide collectors with clues to potential solutions. For example:

"How did you get into this predicament?"

"What caused you to fall behind?"

"Can you put your finger on a particular reason for your payment difficulties?"

"Is there anything we can do to help you get back on track?"

"What are you planning to do to bring your account up to date?"

Fact-finding questions are usually helpful in winning the

customer's cooperation. Customers generally regard inquisitive collectors as helpful and sincere. Inquisitive collectors also get more information, which leads to better, more enforceable agreements.

Reaching an Agreement

The fourth major element of telephone collection calling is reaching an agreement. During this critical phase, the collector must negotiate a payment plan, overcome objections and excuses, and finalize the agreement.

Negotiating a Payment Plan

The goal of every collector is to collect what's due in the shortest time possible. If, during the fact-finding process, it becomes apparent that full and immediate payment is not possible, the collector must go for the next best thing, which is a payment plan. A payment plan is a systematic schedule of partial payments designed to bring a delinquent customer's account up-to-date within a specific amount of time. To successfully negotiate a payment plan, you must:

1. Take control of the situation. Ask for as much as you can get, as fast as you can get it.
2. Sell the benefits of the plan. Your customer must be convinced that the plan is in his or her best interests.
3. Compromise when necessary. There's no point in attempting to force a plan on your customer that he or she would be incapable of honoring.
4. Obtain specific commitments. Precise payment amounts and due dates are a must.

For most delinquent customers the prospect of gaining additional time to meet their obligations is incentive enough to agree to the terms of a mutually beneficial payment plan. Of course, some delinquent customers have no intention of keeping their word. How can a collector know which customers are sincere and which are not? I recommend the use of an immediate good faith payment to bind all payment plans. A payment made by a past-due customer on the day a payment plan is agreed to is an immediate good faith payment. Good faith payments demonstrate a customer's understanding and acceptance of the terms of the agreement. These payments needn't be large, but they must be made as agreed. If the customer fails to meet this initial test of sincerity, you'll know that stronger action is needed. For obvious reasons, it's better to find that out sooner than later.

If the customer accepts your proposed payment plan, you should immediately finalize the agreement. On the other hand, if the customer continues to voice objections to your proposed payment plan, you'll have to find a way to overcome those objections.

Overcoming Objections

If the customer has resisted all your efforts to reach an agreement, you'll have to work even harder to overcome that resistance. By systematically tackling the customer's objections, you'll soon discover whether the customer is sincere about bringing the account up-to-date or whether the customer is stalling for time—or attempting to avoid payment altogether.

The first step in the process of overcoming objections is to find out what the customer is objecting to. To do that, you'll have to break your most recent proposal into smaller, more manageable pieces. You should then submit the pieces of your proposal to the customer one at a time to determine which elements are objectionable and which are not. For example, suppose you're trying to collect a $500 past-due account. You call the customer on May 25 and propose a payment plan that will bring the customer's account up-to-date by July 1. Your payment plan consists of two partial payments: one payment of $250 due June 1 and another payment of $250 due July 1.* Further assume that the customer has told you:

1. That he or she is paid on the fifteenth and the thirtieth of every month.
2. That he or she is not able to pay $250 by June 1 because the May 30 paycheck has already been spent.
3. That he or she will be able to pay the account in full by July 1.

---

*If you are wondering why you shouldn't just ask for payment of $500 by July 1 and forget about the $250 partial payments, remember that you're dealing with a delinquent customer. It wouldn't be smart to wait until July 1 to find out if the customer intends to pay you. Asking for half now and the other half within a month will give you a chance to test the customer's sincerity.

Your first task is to get the customer's promise to have his or her account paid up by July 1. Once you have a commitment on that, you should discuss the other elements of your payment plan. Because the customer has promised to have the account paid in full by July 1, it's fairly obvious that he or she would have no problem paying at least $250 on July 1. The only sticking point is the $250 payment that you have asked for by June 1. When you return to the issue of the June 1 payment, the customer will probably tell you that June 15 is the soonest he or she could possibly make that payment. You will then have to decide whether to change the due date of the first payment to June 15 or whether to make a counter proposal. In this situation it would be wise to ask for a good faith payment of $50 by June 1, payment of $200 by June 15, and payment of $250 on or before July 1. If the customer agrees, you should finalize the agreement.

Remember that to overcome objections you must:

1. Break your payment proposals into smaller, more manageable pieces.
2. Find out what the customer is objecting to.
3. Momentarily set aside the points your customer objects to and obtain agreement on the undisputed points.
4. Return to the disputed points and negotiate solutions to them.

Overcoming Excuses

Not all past-due customers are as accommodating as the customer in our previous example. In fact, some delinquent customers purposely raise objections to buy additional time or escape their responsibilities. These objections are really excuses. Excuses are tricky because they usually have a ring of truth about them. It's impossible to know for sure whether they're actually excuses or legitimate objections until you check them out, which takes time. There's a good reason for taking the time to check them out. If you don't, you could get into trouble. If you assume the customer has given you an excuse and you're wrong, you're likely to lose a customer. If you assume the customer hasn't given you an excuse and you're wrong, you're likely to lose your money.

If a past-due customer presents you with a suspicious payment objection, there are several things you should do:

1. Get all the facts. Listen carefully, ask questions, and take notes.

2. Look for answers. Check your records for information that may be useful in confirming or refuting the customer's story.
3. Get to the bottom of the situation as quickly as possible and report back to the customer. The longer it takes you to resolve the matter, the longer you'll have to wait for your money.
4. Take appropriate action. It is your job to overcome all customer objections whether they are legitimate or not. That means calmly, effectively, intelligently, and systematically dealing with every problem standing in the way of a prompt resolution of the customer's account.

The following are examples of common customer excuses and appropriate collector rebuttals:

Excuse	Response
"We never received a bill."	"What is your address?"

Always follow up by mailing the customer a copy of your invoice. If the customer frequently loses your invoices, send them by certified mail with return receipt requested.

"Our check must have been lost in the mail."	"When did you mail your check, where did you mail it, what is your check number, and how much was the check for?"

If the check has allegedly been in transit more than two weeks, ask your customer to stop payment and send a new check. If a large amount of money is involved, you may want to ask your customer to stop payment and send the money by bank wire transfer.*

---

*A bank wire transfer is a method by which funds can be transferred from one bank account to another. All you need to do is (1) provide your customer with the name, location, and account number of your bank; (2) ask your customer to contact his or her bank to authorize the transfer of funds to your bank; and (3) notify your banker to advise you when the customer's funds are received. Funds can be wire transferred virtually anywhere in the continental United States within a matter of minutes.

> "Your check won't be processed by our computer for another two weeks."

> "Please process our check manually."

If the amount of money is large, ask the customer to send the money by bank wire transfer.

> "I can't pay your $600 bill because all checks totaling more than $500 need two signatures and I'm the only check signer here."

> "Send two checks for $300."

Whatever the limit is, ask for smaller checks that total the amount due.

Finalizing the Agreement

The goal of every telephone collection call is to reach an agreement that brings the customer's account up-to-date within a reasonable period of time. Your job isn't finished, however, until you have properly concluded your collection call. By using the following techniques you'll not only bring your collection calls to an appropriate close, you'll also increase the odds of your agreements being successfully implemented.

1. Summarize the terms of the agreement—After you and the customer have arranged a specific payment agreement, but before you end your telephone conversation, it is essential to restate the terms of the agreement to help eliminate misunderstandings. You must go over all the pertinent details: payment amounts, due dates, method of payment (check, money order, or cash), remittance location, and manner of delivery (mail, hand delivery, or bank wire transfer). It's also advisable to end telephone collection calls on a positive note by expressing your appreciation for the customer's cooperation and by saying something motivational like, "I'm sure you'll rest easier knowing your account will soon be paid up."
2. Confirm the agreement in writing—Every payment arrangement must be confirmed in writing. Your confirmation letter should include the same information covered in your closing summary. For maximum effect, the letter should be sent the same day or the next day after the agreement was reached.

3. Mark your collection file for follow-up—It's important to mark the customer's collection file ahead for follow-up on the appropriate date. It's best to follow up on the due date, unless it's necessary to allow an extra day or two for payment processing. See Part II, chapter 9.
4. Update your records—If you take the time to confirm your agreements in writing, updating your records is as simple as dropping a copy of your confirmation letter into the customer's collection file. While everything is still fresh in your mind you should also take one last look at the notes you took during your telephone conversation. Make sure you know what was said, by whom, and about what. If your notes are incomplete, fill in the gaps now. If your notes are difficult to read, rewrite them now. It's also good to record your impressions of the customer's demeanor. Noting the way the customer reacted to your collection approach will prove useful if further collection measures become necessary.

Following Up

The sixth and final element of a successful telephone collection call is the process of following up. Remember Wolner's Rule: *Words are nice, but action is better.* While obtaining a payment commitment from a past-due customer is an achievement, it is secondary in importance to actually being paid. To insure successful implementation of your payment agreements you must follow up.

Monitoring Compliance

Monitoring compliance means detecting missed payments as soon as they occur and taking swift action to get the customer back on schedule. By monitoring payment due dates and making sure payments are received as agreed, you'll stop negligent customers in their tracks.

Taking Appropriate Action

When customers violate the terms of payment agreements, they must be confronted. At this point, you'll be glad you put the terms of your agreement in writing. To save time, it is preferable to contact negligent customers by telephone. If you're not able to make immediate telephone contact, a letter should be sent.

Customers offer a variety of reasons for not honoring payment agreements. The following tips will help you handle the most common ones:

1. If the customer blatantly refuses to abide by the terms of the agreement or ignores your calls and letters, you should:
   (a) Mail the customer a final demand letter (certified mail with return receipt) requesting immediate payment of the balance on the account; and
   (b) Take stronger action if payment is not made within a reasonable amount of time. See Part III.
2. If the customer claims to have forgotten or misunderstood the terms of the agreement, you should:
   (a) Mail a copy of your confirmation letter (the letter you wrote detailing the terms of the agreement) to the customer, along with a letter requesting full compliance with the terms of the agreement; and
   (b) Take stronger action if missed payments are not received within a reasonable amount of time.
3. If circumstances beyond the customer's control have made it impossible to honor the terms of the agreement, you should:
   (a) Ask the customer to fully explain why he or she is unable to pay as agreed;
   (b) Negotiate a new agreement if everything checks out; and
   (c) Take stronger action to collect the entire balance if the customer is not cooperative.

Faxing

When it comes to collecting money, one of the most exciting developments in the area of telecommunications is the fax machine. The ability to instantly transmit high resolution images of letters, invoices, contracts, and other data to virtually any corner of the globe by picking up the telephone has revolutionized the collection industry. Businesses of all types now depend on fax machines to send and receive important business information. Fax machines allow creditors to avoid the delays associated with mailing copies of missing or disputed invoices to customers. Instead, within moments, creditors have the capability to put both a past due notice and an invoice in the hands of a delinquent customer.

PART III. ALTERNATIVE COLLECTION MEASURES

While most delinquent customers respond to the collection methods outlined in Part II, extraordinary measures will be necessary to bring some of your credit customers to terms. The alternative collection measures presented in Part III are designed to help you handle your toughest collection problems.

WHY ALTERNATIVE COLLECTION MEASURES ARE NEEDED

Almost every company encounters slow-pay and no-pay credit customers. When confronted with such customers, many credit granters give up in frustration or wait too long to begin their efforts. The secret, however, is not to get discouraged. Take problem accounts in stride, react appropriately, and use the knowledge you gain from solving such problems to avoid similar problems in the future. Credit problems don't disappear on their own. The longer they are left alone, the more unwieldly they become. You must take decisive action when you encounter customers who resist your usual collection efforts.

To effectively handle even the most difficult customers, credit granters must know (1) when it would be appropriate to use alternative collection measures, (2) what alternative collection measures are available for use, and (3) how to decide which alternative collection measure to use.

WHEN TO USE ALTERNATIVE COLLECTION MEASURES

The alternative collection measures discussed here should be used only as a last resort. Using these measures too early could be as disasterous as doing so too late. Unfortunately, there is no set formula for deciding when to use alternative collection measures.

Quicker action will be required in some situations than in others. You'll have to use your own best judgment. Most credit professionals agree, however, that delinquent accounts should be resolved before they become ninety days past-due. If you haven't received payment or arranged a specific payment plan by then, alternative collection measures are strongly suggested.

THE OPTIONS

The following is a brief description of the chapters on specific alternative collection measures discussed in Part III:

1. Settlements—This chapter helps credit granters decide when it's advisable to settle an account for less than the balance owing, how to arrive at a settlement amount, what form your settlement offer should take, and why the timing of your offer is so important.
2. Small claims court—This chapter covers the process of deciding whether or not to file suit in small claims court and the specifics of filing suit, appearing in court, and obtaining and collecting judgments.
3. Collection agencies—This chapter explains when it is appropriate to use collection agencies, what you should know before you select a collection agency, how you can protect yourself from unscrupulous collection agencies, and what it will cost to use a collection agency.
4. Collection attorneys—This chapter advises credit granters on selecting a competent collection attorney, determining the role the attorney will play, figuring out what it will cost to retain the services of a collection attorney, and reacting appropriately if you're dissatisfied with the attorney you select.
5. Alternative dispute resolution—This chapter describes the two primary forms of alternative dispute resolution, mediation and arbitration, when they should be used, how they work, and their applicability in collecting money.

CHOOSING AN ALTERNATIVE COLLECTION MEASURE

To decide which alternative collection measure to use, it's important to consider:

1. The cost involved—Settlements, small claims court, and alternative dispute resolution are generally more economical than other alternative collection measures because you'll end up doing most of the work yourself. Collection agencies and collection attorneys are usually quite expensive because they're doing most of the work for you.
2. The amount of time you're willing to invest—Some alternative collection measures will require more of your time than others. If you don't have the time to work out settlements, to file suit and obtain a judgment in small claims court, or to engage in mediation or arbitration sessions, you may have no choice but to retain the services of a third-party debt collector.
3. The risk and benefits—There are times when it would be wise to avoid adversarial proceedings. For example, if you're having trouble collecting from an established customer, it would be advisable to attempt to settle, mediate, or arbitrate the account. Filing a lawsuit or engaging the services of a collection agency in this situation could destroy a profitable business relationship.

CHAPTER 13
SETTLEMENTS

There are three situations in which credit granters should seriously consider settling an account for less than the amount due:

1. When you're at odds with a good customer—Remember the adage, "The customer is always right." If something has happened to damage an otherwise prosperous business relationship, proposing an adjustment in the customer's bill may help repair the damage.
2. When your options are limited—Remember that "discretion is the better part of valor." If the amount owed is very small, further collection efforts may be impractical. If you're having trouble locating sufficient assets to levy against, legal action may be futile. If your customer's financial condition is shaky, delaying a resolution to the problem may be calamitous. Under these or similar circumstances it would be prudent to seek a settlement.
3. When it's beneficial to settle—Abraham Lincoln once said, "Never stir up [needless] litigation." If you're able to resolve your differences with a customer without resorting to the use of third-party debt collectors, you'll probably end up saving time and money.

ARRIVING AT A SETTLEMENT OFFER

Your settlement offer should be in direct proportion to (1) the importance of preserving the customer's business, (2) the likelihood of collecting if you are unable to settle the account, and (3) the amount of time, money, and effort it would take you to pursue the full balance.

If it's important to retain the customer's business, it's unlikely that any other alternative collection measures would be effective in resolving the customer's account, or it's going to cost you a substantial amount of time, money, and effort to pursue the full balance, you'll obviously be willing to give up more than if the reverse were true. A routine evaluation of your most serious past-due accounts in relation to these three criteria will help you arrive at a realistic settlement offer.

STRUCTURE

When making settlement offers, you should:

1. Put your settlement offer in writing;
2. Make sure the customer understands that your settlement offer will be withdrawn if payment of the proposed amount is not received by a specific date; and
3. Spell out the benefits of the customer's acceptance of your settlement offer.

You must convince your customer that your settlement offer is your final attempt to reach an amicable resolution of the problem. If the customer fails to accept your settlement offer (or a mutually agreed upon counteroffer), you should send a final demand letter requesting payment of the original balance.

TIMING

Unless you properly set the stage for your settlement offer, you run the risk of jeopardizing its acceptance. If you haven't made a serious attempt to collect the full amount owing or you seem too eager to settle, your customer may hold out for a better offer. If, however, your approach has been harsh or abusive, it may be too late to win the customer's cooperation at any price.

There are two important rules to follow in deciding when to propose a settlement. Settlement offers should always: (1) follow a serious attempt to collect the full amount due, and (2) precede the threat of more forceful collection action.

A PRACTICAL EXAMPLE

Leading up to a settlement offer can be awkward. Credit granters must appear to be willing but not overly anxious to settle. Past-due customers must be led, not pushed, in the direction of a settlement. Here's a tactic that I have used successfully to initiate settlement offers: First, write a letter to the affected customer stating that your books are being audited. Explain that your accountant has recommended placement of the customer's account with a professional debt collector before the end of the current fiscal year, but that you have decided to give the customer one last chance to clear things up. Carefully describe the terms of your proposed settlement in your letter. Let the customer know how much money is to be paid, in what form (cash, money order, certified check, bank wire transfer, company or personal check), to whom, and by what date. Finally, make sure the customer understands that your offer is a one-time-only proposition and that payment of the amended amount must be received by a specific date or the deal is off. If the customer accepts your settlement offer and pays as agreed, remember to clear the remaining balance from your books. If the customer fails to accept your settlement offer, send a final demand letter and take appropriate action to collect your money.

Because no one knows when you close your books, you can send similar letters at any time during the year.

DECIDING WHETHER TO SETTLE

Credit granters have a right to expect their customers to pay as agreed. It is disturbing to have to settle for less than a customer owes you. There are times, however, when credit granters must put more emphasis on expedience than on principle. If you stand to lose more by pursuing a delinquent account than by settling, it makes sense to settle.

In deciding whether or not to make a settlement offer, consider the following:

1. A settlement should be proposed only as a last resort when your usual collection measures have proved unsuccessful in resolving an account.
2. A settlement should be proposed only when it is in the best interests of the credit granter.
3. A settlement should be proposed only when there is reason to believe the customer is ready, willing, and able to accept it.

TWO FINAL POINTS

First, remember that "it takes two to tango." Your customer may reject your settlement offer despite the fact that it is in his or her best interests. You must then be prepared to either proceed with more forceful collection action or give up. Second, there are times when it is in the best interests of a credit granter to put more emphasis on principle than expedience. By selectively pursuing some of your less promising accounts, you'll send a signal to the rest of your customers that you are serious about enforcing the terms of your credit policy.

CHAPTER 14
SMALL CLAIMS COURT

The concept of small claims court dates back to the early 1900s. Small claims courts were established for two reasons: (1) to give ordinary citizens access to the judicial system, and (2) to relieve the traditional court system of an ever-growing number of small-dollar lawsuits.

There is some difference of opinion over what constitutes a "small" claim. The rules that govern the various small claims courts across the United States are set by state or local statute. Jurisdictional limits vary widely across the country.° Table 3 lists state filing limits at the time of publication.

FILING REQUIREMENTS

Anyone of legal age is entitled to bring a lawsuit in small claims court. In most jurisdictions individuals are free to enter small claims court without benefit of legal counsel.°° In fact, small claims courts were designed to allow people without legal knowledge to come before the court and explain what happened in their own words.

As already stated, the amount of money you can sue for in small claims court is limited by statute. If your claim exceeds the statutory limit, however, you are free to waive your claim to the amount of money in excess of the statutory limit and bring your suit into small claims court.

°Many states are raising maximum small claims court awards to adjust for inflation and stimulate greater use of small claims court to relieve backlogs in the traditional court system. For example, Minnesota will raise its limit to $7,500 July 1994.

°°Many jurisdictions limit attorney participation, and others bar such participation altogether.

Before filing suit, the person or company suing (the plaintiff) must make sure the person or company being sued (the defendant) lives, works, or operates a business in the area served by the small claims court where the case will be heard. In other words, you must be certain that the small claims court where you file suit has jurisdiction over the defendant.

DECIDING WHETHER TO USE SMALL CLAIMS COURT

Credit granters should use small claims court only as a last resort. In fact, there are a number of things you must do before you decide to file suit in small claims court:

1. Assemble all the information you have. Double check all your facts. Locate and insert copies of letters, invoices, cancelled checks, and phone records into your collection file.
2. If you're suing an individual, make sure you have the person's correct name and address and the correct name and address of the person's employer. If you're suing a company, call the branch of your state or local government that governs the incorporation, licensing, or registration of businesses. Obtain the company's exact legal name, the names of principal owners and officers, the company's address, and any other pertinent information. This is important because your case could be thrown out of court if you incorrectly identify the defendant.
3. Find out whether the party you're suing has assets (income, bank accounts, or real property) to satisfy your claim should you be successful in obtaining a judgment. If the person you're suing has no assets, obtaining a judgment against him or her could be an exercise in futility. Even if the defendant has assets, the court won't take action unless and until the plaintiff finds those assets and notifies the court of their location. Only then will you be able to attach the defendant's assets to satisfy your judgment.

If you have taken the preceding steps and you're still committed to filing suit in small claims court, first make a formal demand for payment. Send the delinquent customer a certified letter with return receipt and address correction requested. Give the customer one last chance to come to terms with you and avoid legal action. You should wait a reasonable amount of time for a response (seven to ten days is sufficient). If the delinquent customer fails to respond, refuses to accept delivery of your letter, or declines to agree to a plan that will bring the account up-to-date, you should immediately file suit. It is very important to keep a copy of your final demand for payment, as well as the green card the post office will return to you following delivery or attempted delivery of your letter. This is important for four reasons:

1. If the past-due customer accepts delivery of your letter and signs the green card, you'll have proof that you properly notified the customer of his or her obligation and that you gave the customer an opportunity to resolve the matter amicably.
2. If the delinquent customer refuses to accept delivery of your letter, the mail carrier will note the customer's refusal on the green card. This will prove that you attempted to notify the customer in good faith. It will also confirm the fact that you have the customer's correct address.
3. If the past-due customer has moved but has left a forwarding address, the post office will deliver your letter and notify you of the new delivery address.
4. If the delinquent customer has moved and left no forwarding address, the post office will return your letter. You should keep the unopened letter as proof of your attempt to notify the customer in good faith.

If you are unable to locate the past-due customer's current home address, you should attempt to notify the customer at work. If the customer's employer is unknown, you'll have to use "skiptracing" techniques to locate the customer's current address or the name and address of his or her employer. You will not be able to file suit without this information. See appendix E.

FILING SUIT

Before filing suit in small claims court, the plaintiff must review the evidence contained in the delinquent customer's collection file. It is then advisable to prepare a brief written explanation of what happened, indicating specific dates, amounts, names, and so forth. When you're sure of your facts, it's time to actually file your claim. Most jurisdictions allow aggrieved parties to file their claims either in person or by mail. To schedule your case for a hearing it will be necessary to (1) pay a nominal filing fee (usually not more than ten dollars), and (2) fill out a claim form similar to the one in figure 15.* When you fill out your claim form, you'll be asked to accurately identify the party you're suing and explain your reason for filing suit. You'll also be required to specify the dollar amount of your claim. To keep all this straight, it's a good idea to have your collection file handy as you complete your claim form. When you're finished filling out your claim form, you'll have to sign it and swear, in the presence of a court deputy or notary public, that the information you have provided is true.

NOTIFICATION OF THE PARTIES

Depending on the case load in the jurisdiction in which you file suit, it may be several weeks or perhaps several months before your case will be scheduled for trial. The court will select a trial date and put the case on the court calendar. If the plaintiff files suit in person, he or she will be advised of the trial date verbally at the time of filing. If the plaintiff files suit by mail, he or she will be advised of the trial date by mail.

A summons and notice of trial will be mailed to the defendant by first class or certified mail. If the post office returns the defendant's notice of trial because the defendant has moved and left no forwarding address, it will be the plaintiff's responsibility to provide the court with a new address. Otherwise, the case will be dismissed "without prejudice," meaning the plaintiff may refile when a proper address is found. If the defendant's residence is not known, but his or her place of employment is, the plaintiff may serve a personal summons on the defendant at work. Check with the small claims court in your jurisdiction to find out what you need to do to serve the defendant personally.

COUNTERCLAIMS

Upon receiving notice of trial, the defendant may decide to file a claim against the plaintiff, which is known as a counterclaim. The procedure for filing a counterclaim is nearly identical to the

---

*Some jurisdictions have a variety of claim forms to choose from: general form, goods sold/services rendered form, replevin form (to obtain the return of goods), and auto accident form. A goods sold/services rendered form would be the normal choice for a credit granter.

FIGURE 15
SMALL CLAIMS COURT CLAIM FORM

STATE OF MINNESOTA

COUNTY OF HENNEPIN

HC 4327 - General Claim (7/93)
CONCILIATION COURT
857C Government Center
Minneapolis, MN 55487

_____
_____
_____
                                      Plaintiff(s)

Address _____

Daytime Phone: _____
                  versus

_____
_____
_____
                                  Defendant(s)

Address: _____

Claim Amount
including fee _____

Counterclaim
including fee _____

Case No _____

Statement of Claim

Plaintiff alleges that defendant is indebted to the plaintiff in the amount of $_____ plus $18.00 (or $28.00) filing fee, by reason of the following facts:

_____

_____

(Execute affidavit of plaintiff's claim on reverse side)

Statement of Counterclaim

Defendant alleges that plaintiff is indebted to the defendant in the amount of $_____ , plus $18.00 (or $28.00) filing fee, by reason of the following facts:

_____

_____

(Execute affidavit of defendant's counterclaim on reverse side)

Proceedings

For trial on	_____ at _____	Room _____	Notice mailed _____	
Continued to	_____ at _____	Room _____	Notice mailed _____	
Continued to	_____ at _____	Room _____	Notice mailed _____	
Continued to	_____ at _____	Room _____	Notice mailed _____	
Reopened for	_____ at _____	Room _____	Notice mailed _____	Costs $_____

Judgment for Plaintiff / Defendant by default for $_____ mailed _____ Ref. _____

Judgment for Plaintiff / Defendant by default for $_____ mailed _____ Ref. _____

Dismissed NAP _____   Stricken _____   Settled _____

State of Minnesota
County of Hennepin

Affidavit of Plaintiff's Claim

_____ swears/affirms: That __he is _____ the plaintiff(s) named; that the Statement of Claim on the reverse is true of h___ own knowledge; that defendant(s) is not now in the military or naval service of the United States.

Subscribed and (sworn to)(affirmed under penalties of perjury) before me

on _____, 19_____ .   Signed_____

_____   Phone_____
Court Deputy or Notary

State of Minnesota
County of Hennepin

Affidavit of Defendant's Counterclaim

_____ swears/affirms: That __he is _____ the defendant(s) named; that the Statement of Counterclaim on the reverse is true of h___ own knowledge; that plaintiff(s) is not now in the military or naval service of the United States.

Subscribed and (sworn to)(affirmed under penalties of perjury) before me

on _____, 19_____ .   Signed_____

_____   Phone_____
Court Deputy or Notary

Certificate and Order on Removal

Removal to District Court having been demanded, I certify that the foregoing is the record of proceedings had, the issues tried and the order entered in this action and I hereby vacate the order for judgment.

Dated_____, 19_____   _____
                                                            Conciliation Court Judge

---

Transcript Issued to District Court

Dated_____, 19_____   Signed_____

procedure for filing a claim. The defendant will be required to pay a fee and fill out a form. See figure 15. Defendants are usually required to file their counterclaims at least one week before the trial to allow the court time to notify the plaintiff. The defendant's counterclaim will be heard by the court at the same time the plaintiff's claim is scheduled to be heard.

APPEARING IN COURT

As most credit granters know, defendants don't always show up in court. Nevertheless, the plaintiff must be present. During your court appearance it's important to

1. Be on time. If you're late, your case may be dismissed. You could even lose the case if the defendant has filed a counterclaim against you.
2. Be prepared. Bring all your evidence to the trial. If you have witnesses to testify in your favor, make sure they come to the trial. If necessary, the court will assist you in subpoenaing witnesses.
3. Be brief. Your presentation of the facts should be short and to the point.
4. Be respectful. Remember that you're in a court of law. Address the judge, referee, or arbitrator as "your honor."
5. Be reserved. Don't lose your temper, and don't interrupt the defendant or witnesses while they are speaking. You'll be given ample opportunity to tell your side of the story and to question the defendant's testimony. Wait your turn.

FAILING TO APPEAR

If the defendant doesn't show up but the plaintiff does, the plaintiff will be expected to provide the court with sufficient evidence to support his or her claim. If everything is in order, the court will enter a default judgment in favor of the plaintiff. If the plaintiff fails to appear but the defendant does, the plaintiff's case will be dismissed. However, if the defendant has filed a counterclaim and does appear, a default judgment may be entered against the plaintiff.

NOTIFICATION OF A DECISION

The parties are usually notified of a decision by mail seven to ten days after the trial. The judgment of the court will specify the

winner of the case and the amount of the judgment. There will be an automatic stay (a brief delay) before the judgment becomes official to allow the parties time to appeal or vacate the judgment.*
In all but default cases, parties who are dissatisfied with small claims court judgments may appeal to a higher court. Proper notice of appeal, however, must be filed before the date the small claims court judgment becomes official. Appeal procedures are generally more complex than those for the original filing. As a result, it is advisable for appealing parties to be represented by competent legal counsel.

COLLECTING A JUDGMENT

The notice of judgment will instruct the losing party (the judgment debtor) to pay the amount of the judgment entered in favor of the prevailing party (the judgment creditor). The judgment debtor will be asked to do so on or before the date the judgment becomes official. If the judgment debtor pays the court by check on or before the date the judgment becomes official, the court will wait until the check clears the bank. A cashier's check for the amount of the judgment will then be mailed to the judgment creditor by the court, and a notation will be placed in court records indicating that the judgment has been satisfied.

If the judgment creditor receives a check directly from the judgment debtor, he or she should:

1. Double check the amount of the check to be certain it includes the filing fee and any other legally recoverable fees;
2. Cash the check if the amount is correct and wait for the check to clear the bank;
3. Provide the judgment debtor with a satisfaction of judgment. See figure 16; and
4. Notify the court that the judgment has been satisfied.

Remember that once you provide a satisfaction of judgment, the judgment debtor is off the hook.

---

*Most jurisdictions allow default judgments to be set aside, or vacated, only if the absent plaintiff or defendant is able to prove to the court that his or her absence was unintentional or unavoidable.

FIGURE 16
SATISFACTION OF JUDGMENT

State of Minnesota
COUNTY

District Court
JUDICIAL DISTRICT   CASE NO.

SATISFACTION OF JUDGMENT

_____ Plaintiff(s)

vs.

_____ Defendant(s)

PARTIAL SATISFACTION

I, _____, the undersigned judgment creditor hereby certify that judgment in the amount of $_____ which was entered in this Court on _____, 19____, in favor of _____ and against _____ is partially satisfied in the following amounts:

Date Collected	Total Collected	Credit/Costs	Credit/Interest	Credit/Principal

and the Court Administrator shall record the same.

FULL SATISFACTION

I, _____, the undersigned judgment creditor hereby certify that judgment in the amount of $_____ which was entered in this Court on _____, 19____, in favor of _____ and against _____ is fully satisfied and the Court Administrator shall record the same.

Subscribed and sworn to before me on
_____, 19____

_____
Notary Public/Deputy

_____
Signature of Creditor or Creditor's Attorney

EXECUTING A JUDGMENT

As mentioned earlier, you can only attach assets the judgment debtor has. If you did your homework before filing suit, you probably already know where the judgment debtor works or banks. If you didn't, you'll have to locate assets to levy against. By examining your collection file for cancelled checks, looking at the customer's credit application for employment, bank, or property ownership information, and contacting people the judgment debtor knows, you may be able to locate assets. Depending on the laws of your state, some assets may be exempt from judgment execution. This is especially true of wages. Your search for assets should continue until you have found sufficient non-exempt assets to satisfy your judgment. If you are unable to locate a bank account or attachable wages, and you believe the judgment debtor has non-exempt assets, some states provide a procedure to assist judgment debtors in obtaining financial disclosure.*

The procedure to seize non-exempt assets in the jurisdiction where you obtained your judgment generally works like this:

1. Obtain an official transcript (written record) of your judgment from the court. There may be a nominal fee.
2. File the transcript along with an affidavit of identification (known as docketing) with the clerk of civil court where you obtained your judgment, indicating whether you are seeking to attach wages or other property belonging to the judgment debtor. See figure 17A.
3. Obtain a writ of execution, a document that allows you to enforce your judgment. See figure 17B.
4. Take the writ of execution, which specifies exactly where the judgment debtor's assets are, to the sheriff in the jurisdiction where the judgment debtor's assets are located (in this case, the same jurisdiction in which you obtained your judgment). Before levying against the judgment debtor's assets, the sheriff may ask you to provide a modest, nonrefundable deposit to cover time and mileage. At your direction, the sheriff will then serve the execution as many times as it takes to collect your money. Each time the sheriff levies against the judgment debtor's assets, the judgment creditor will be billed for time and mileage by the sheriff's office. The sheriff's fees, however, and all other legally recoverable fees, may be added to the judgment you are attempting to collect.

---

*In Minnesota a judgment creditor must wait 30 days after a judgment has been entered in District Court to request the court to order the judgment debtor to fill out a financial disclosure form. See figure 17C.

FIGURE 17A
AFFIDAVIT OF IDENTIFICATION OF JUDGMENT DEBTOR

State of Minnesota

COUNTY

COURT

JUDICIAL DISTRICT   CASE NO.

_____
_____
_____
                    Plaintiff
         vs.

_____
_____
_____
                    Defendant

AFFIDAVIT OF IDENTIFICATION OF JUDGMENT DEBTOR

_____ being duly sworn on
NAME OF JUDGMENT CREDITOR OR JUDGMENT CREDITOR'S AGENT OR ATTORNEY
oath says; that ____ he is the Judgment Creditor, or the _____ for the
                                                          AGENT OR ATTORNEY
Judgment Creditor, that to the best of h ____ knowledge, information, and belief, the full name(s) of the Judgment Debtor(s) in the action above entitled is as follows:

that the business and occupation of said judgment debtor(s) is as follows:

that the place(s) of residence of said judgment debtor(s) is as follows:

that the place(s) of business of said judgment debtor(s) is as follows:

that the post office address(es) of said judgment debtor(s) is as follows:

| NOTARY STAMP OR COURT SEAL | SUBSCRIBED AND SWORN BEFORE ME ON: DATE: _____ _____ SIGNATURE | THE ABOVE STATEMENT OF CLAIM IS TRUE AND CORRECT TO THE BEST OF MY KNOWLEDGE. SIGNATURE _____ TELEPHONE _____ |

NOTE: If debtor is in an incorporated place of more than 5,000, street and number of both residence and business must be given.

FIGURE 17B
WRIT OF EXECUTION

TITLE		
	State of Minnesota	**WRIT OF EXECUTION** (Personal Property or Money Only)
	COURT	NO.
	COUNTY	JUDICIAL DISTRICT
	DATE JUDGMENT ENTERED	COURT OF ORIGINAL ENTRY
	DATE DOCKETED	TIME DOCKETED
	COUNTY WHERE JUDGMENT ROLL OR TRANSCRIPT FILED	ORIGINAL AMOUNT OF JUDGMENT

THE STATE OF MINNESOTA TO THE SHERIFF OF _____ COUNTY:

  WHEREAS, Judgment was entered in favor of _____

and against _____

  THEREFORE, you are hereby commanded to satisfy said judgment, with interest and your fees, out of the personal property of the judgment debtor(s) within your county on the day when said judgment was docketed in your county, or at any time thereafter not exceeding ten years from the date of entry. You are also required to return this execution within sixty days after its receipt by you to the Clerk of Court named herein.

Amount to be collected:		WITNESS	
Judgment (Amount actually due)	$_____	DATE EXECUTION ISSUED	
Interest from: _____ (date)	_____		
Execution Fee	_____	CLERK OF COURT	*COURT SEAL*
Service Charges	_____		
Other_____	_____	BY DEPUTY	
	_____		
TOTAL	$_____	ENDORSED (JUDGMENT CREDITOR OR ATTORNEY)	

Return of Service

Service Returned By (Check One) ☐ Sheriff ☐ Attorney (MSA. 550.041)

Service Returned (Check One)

☐ Satisfied In Full

☐ Partially Satisfied (Amount Collected) $_____
    (Less Sheriff's Fees) $_____
    (Amount Satisfied) $_____

☐ No Property Found: (I hereby certify and return that I have made diligent search and inquiry in my county and have been unable to find any personal property out of which to satisfy the judgment described in this execution.)

SIGNATURE OF SHERIFF OR ATTORNEY ON RETURN   COUNTY   DATE RETURNED

DATE RETURNED AND FILED WITH CLERK OF COURTS

FIGURE 17C
REQUEST FOR ORDER FOR DISCLOSURE

State of Minnesota	District Court
County	Judicial District	Case No.

_____
_____
_____ Plaintiff
          vs.
_____
_____
_____ Defendant

REQUEST FOR ORDER FOR DISCLOSURE

TO: THE COURT ADMINISTRATOR CONCERNING:

_____
JUDGMENT DEBTOR'S NAME

_____
Address

_____
City/State   Zip

The JUDGMENT CREDITOR states that:
1. The JUDGMENT CREDITOR has won a Judgment in this lawsuit against the JUDGMENT DEBTOR in Conciliation Court.
2. The Court Administrator recorded the Judgment in the official judgment docket more than thirty (30) days ago,
3. The JUDGMENT DEBTOR has not paid all of the money which is owed to the JUDGMENT CREDITOR, and
4. The JUDGMENT CREDITOR and the JUDGMENT DEBTOR have not agreed to some other way to settle the debt.

The JUDGMENT CREDITOR REQUESTS that the Court order the JUDGMENT DEBTOR to fill out a Financial Disclosure form, and mail it to the JUDGMENT CREDITOR at the address shown below.

The statements made in this request are true and correct to the best of my knowledge.

Date: _____

_____
JUDGMENT CREDITOR'S Authorized signature and title

_____
Print JUDGMENT CREDITOR'S Name

_____
Address

_____
City/State   Zip

_____
Telephone

5. If you are attempting to attach wages, it will be necessary to obtain and serve a garnishment exemption notice on the judgment debtor at his or her home address. This gives the judgment debtor an opportunity to exclude certain income from attachment. See figure 18. If the judgment debtor fails to respond to the garnishment exemption notice within a specific number of days, a summons may be served on the judgment debtor's employer. The employer will then be obliged to disclose the judgment debtor's income to the sheriff. The judgment creditor is then free to execute on the judgment debtor's wages.

If the judgment debtor's assets are located in a jurisdiction within the state other than the one where your judgment was obtained, substitute the following step for number two above: File the transcript with the clerk of civil court in the jurisdiction where you obtained your judgment. Advise the clerk of civil court that you wish to transfer your judgment to the appropriate state court to levy on the judgment debtor's assets in another jurisdiction within the state. Then file the transcript with the appropriate state court.

WHEN ASSETS CANNOT BE LOCATED

In most jurisdictions small claims court judgments are valid for seven to ten years. During this time unsatisfied judgments become a lien on real or personal property the judgment debtor owns or acquires. Unsatisfied judgments also find their way into consumer and commercial credit reports, making it difficult for judgment debtors to obtain credit. A judgment will also put you in a better position if the judgment debtor later declares bankruptcy. When the petitioner's assets are distributed you'll have a preference over unsecured creditors without judgments. Thus, even if the person you're suing in small claims court lacks or appears to lack attachable assets, he or she may eventually settle with you in order to (1) obtain credit or remove derogatory information from a credit file or (2) sell property or obtain clear title to property on which you have a lien.

SHOULD YOU USE SMALL CLAIMS COURT?

Pursuing a claim in small claims court requires a substantial commitment on the part of the credit granter. It'll take time to file your claim, prepare your case, appear in court, and collect your judgment. If the person you're suing lives, works, or operates a

FIGURE 18
GARNISHMENT EXEMPTION NOTICE

STATE OF MINNESOTA   DISTRICT COURT
COUNTY OF _____   _____ JUDICIAL DISTRICT

_____
(Creditor)

against

_____   GARNISHMENT EXEMPTION NOTICE
(Debtor)   AND NOTICE OF INTENT TO GARNISH
        EARNINGS WITHIN TEN DAYS

and

_____
(Garnishee)

THE STATE OF MINNESOTA
TO THE ABOVE NAMED DEBTOR

    PLEASE TAKE NOTICE that a garnishment summons or levy may be served upon your employer or other third parties, without any further court proceedings or notice to you, ten days or more from the date hereof. Some or all of your earnings are exempt from garnishment. If your earnings are garnished, your employer must show you how the amount that is garnished from your earnings was calculated. You have the right to request a hearing if you claim the garnishment is incorrect.

    Your earnings are completely exempt from garnishment if you are now a recipient of relief based on need, if you have been a recipient of relief within the last six months, or if you have been an inmate of a correctional institution in the last six months.

    Relief based on need includes Aid to Families with Dependent Children (AFDC), AFDC-Emergency Assistance (AFDC-EA), Medical Assistance (MA), General Assistance (GA), General Assistance Medical Care (GAMC), Emergency General Assistance (EGA), Work Readiness, Minnesota Supplemental Aid (MSA), MSA Emergency Assistance (MSA-EA), Supplemental Security Income (SSI), and Energy Assistance.

    If you wish to claim an exemption, you should fill out the appropriate form below, sign it, and send it to the creditor's attorney and the garnishee.

    You may wish to contact the attorney for the creditor in order to arrange for a settlement of the debt or contact an attorney to advise you about exemptions or other rights.

PENALTIES

    (1) Be advised that even if you claim an exemption, a garnishment summons may still be served on your employer. If your earnings are garnished after you claim an exemption, you may petition the court for a determination of your exemption. If the court finds that the creditor disregarded your claim of exemption in bad faith, you will be entitled to costs, reasonable attorney fees, actual damages, and an amount not to exceed $100.

    (2) HOWEVER, BE WARNED if you claim an exemption, the creditor can also petition the court for a determination of your exemption, and if the court finds that you claimed an exemption in bad faith, you will be assessed costs and reasonable attorney's fees plus an amount not to exceed $100.

    (3) If after receipt of this notice, you in bad faith take action to frustrate the garnishment, thus requiring the creditor to petition the court to resolve the problem, you will be liable to the creditor for costs and reasonable attorney's fees plus an amount not to exceed $100.

DATED: _____   _____
                                                      (Attorney for) Creditor

                                                           _____

                                                           _____
                                                                           Address

                                                           _____
                                                                           Telephone

DEBTOR'S EXEMPTION CLAIM NOTICE

I hereby claim that my earnings are exempt from garnishment because:

(1) I am presently a recipient of relief based on need. (Specify the program, case number, and the county from which relief is being received.)

_____ _____ _____
Program   Case Number (if known)   County

(2) I am not now receiving relief based on need, but I have received relief based on need within the last six months. (Specify the program, case number, and the county from which relief has been received.)

_____ _____ _____
Program   Case Number (if known)   County

(3) I have been an inmate of a correctional institution within the last six months. (Specify the correctional institution and location.)

_____ _____
Correctional Institution   Location

I hereby authorize any agency that has distributed relief to me or any correctional institution in which I was an inmate to disclose to the above-named creditor or his attorney only whether or not I am or have been a recipient of relief based on need or an inmate of a correctional institution within the last six months. I have mailed or delivered a copy of this form to the creditor or creditor's attorney.

_____   _____
Date   Debtor

                                        _____

                                        _____
                                        Address

business in a jurisdiction that is far from where you are, the amount of time and money you'll be required to invest in travel alone may be prohibitive. You'll also have to spend time sitting in court waiting for your case to be called. In addition, you could end up waiting a long time for your case to come to trial. If so, you might be better off using one of the other alternative collection measures.

On the other hand, many credit granters have found small claims court to be an effective way to handle small-dollar delinquent accounts, and it's relatively inexpensive.

TABLE 3
SMALL CLAIMS COURT JURISDICTIONAL LIMITS

State	Limit	State	Limit
Alabama	$ 1,500	Nebraska	$ 1,800
Alaska	$ 5,000	Nevada	$ 2,500
Arizona	$ 1,000	New Hampshire	$ 2,500
Arkansas	$ 3,000	New Jersey	$ 1,000
California	$ 5,000	New Mexico	$ 5,000
Colorado	$ 2,000	New York	$ 2,000
Connecticut	$ 2,000	North Carolina	$ 3,000
Deleware	$ 2,500	North Dakota	$ 2,000
Florida	$10,000	Ohio	$ 2,000
Georgia	$ 5,000	Oklahoma	$ 3,000
Hawaii	$ 2,500	Oregon	$ 2,500
Idaho	$ 2,000	Pennsylvania	$ 5,000
Illinois	$ 2,500	Rhode Island	$ 1,500
Indiana	$ 3,000	South Carolina	$ 2,500
Iowa	$ 2,000	South Dakota	$ 2,000
Kansas	$ 1,000	Tennessee	$10,000**
Kentucky	$ 1,500	Texas	$ 2,500
Louisiana	$ 2,000	Utah	$ 1,000
Maine	$ 1,400	Vermont	$ 2,000
Maryland	$ 2,500	Virginia	$ 1,000
Massachusetts	$ 1,500	Washington	$ 2,000
Michigan	$ 1,500	Washington D.C.	$ 2,000
Minnesota	$ 6,000*	West Virginia	$ 3,000
Mississippi	$ 1,000	Wisconsin	$ 2,000
Missouri	$ 1,500	Wyoming	$ 2,000
Montana	$ 2,500		

*Minnesota's jurisdictional limit will increase to $7,500 July 1994
**Tennessee's jurisdictional limit is $15,000 if population of county where action is brought is more than 700,000.

CHAPTER 15
COLLECTION AGENCIES

Many credit granters turn to collection agencies when they run out of time or patience in dealing with past-due customers. By placing accounts with a collection agency, credit granters are able to use their time more profitably. Collection agency fees are steep, but collection agencies do offer credit granters certain advantages over some of the other alternative collection measures. For one thing, collection agency users have a firm idea of what it will cost to recover their money. Also, fees are usually due only if money is actually recovered.

This chapter will help you select a collection agency by explaining when it would be appropriate to use collection agencies; why you must select the right type of collection agency; what you need to know before you select a collection agency; and how you can protect yourself from unscrupulous collection agencies.

WHEN TO USE A COLLECTION AGENCY

Companies turn to collection agencies when they:

1. Lack sufficient time to pursue accounts that are seriously past-due.
2. Lack sufficient "know-how" to pursue accounts that are seriously past-due.
3. Lack sufficient resources (people, equipment, and cash) to pursue accounts that are seriously past-due.

There is no magic formula for determining how long you should wait before turning an account over to a third-party debt collector. Such decisions are usually governed by company policy and the peculiar circumstances of each delinquent account. Remember, however, that most credit professionals agree that delinquent accounts should be resolved before they become ninety days past-due. If you haven't received payment or nailed down a specific payment arrangement by then, alternative collection measures are strongly suggested.

SELECTING THE RIGHT TYPE

There are three different types of collection agencies:

1. Those specializing in the collection of retail accounts—debts arising from the sale of products and services to individual consumers for their personal use.
2. Those specializing in the collection of commercial accounts—debts arising from the sale of products and services to companies or individuals for business use.
3. Those that collect both retail and commercial accounts.

The type of collection agency you need depends on the nature of your business and the type of accounts you're interested in placing. Retail accounts should be placed with retail collection agencies and commercial accounts with commercial collection agencies. If you have both retail and commercial accounts to place, use two separate collection agencies—one to handle your retail accounts and one to handle your commercial accounts. This is important for two reasons:

1. The methods used to collect retail and commercial accounts are quite different. Retail accounts have always been pursued more aggressively than commercial accounts.
2. The laws governing the collection of retail and commercial accounts are quite different. Retail collection methods are strictly regulated by the Fair Debt Collection Practices Act and commercial collection methods are not. See appendix F.

There is a possibility that collectors who switch back and forth between retail and commercial accounts will get their collection methods confused which could lessen the collection agency's effectiveness and reduce recoveries. Also, there is a danger that collectors who collect both retail and commercial accounts will fail to abide by the appropriate legal requirements, which could get both you and the collection agency in trouble. Some collection agencies have tried to get around this problem by hiring separate collectors to handle retail and commercial accounts. But few collection agencies have sufficient resources to maintain two separate collection departments. Unless you can find such an agency, use only collection agencies that specialize in handling either retail or commercial accounts, not both.

BEFORE MAKING A SELECTION

You must do your homework before selecting a collection agency. Unfortunately, many companies blindly pick the collection agencies they use out of the yellow pages, which is a dangerous way to select a collection agency. The following tips will help you select a collection agency that closely matches your needs:

1. Get to know the people with whom you will be working. More specifically, get to know the people who manage the collection agency and those who will be handling your accounts. Ask questions about their experience and education. Remember that the collection agency you choose is acting on your behalf. You owe it to yourself to find out all you can about prospective agencies and their employees.
2. Determine whether the collection agency shields its clients from lawsuits caused by the mistakes of the collection agency or its employees. Reputable collection agencies carry "errors and omissions" insurance to indemnify customers against loss. If the collection agency you're considering claims to have such coverage, ask for a copy of the insurance policy. Verify the effective dates of the policy and the amount of protection afforded.
3. Most states regulate collection agencies. See appendix G. You should check with the collection agency licensing authorities in your state to determine:
    (a) If the agency is licensed;
    (b) If the agency is bonded, and if so, for how much;
    (c) If the agency has ever had its license suspended or revoked, or if any of the agency's owners or officers have ever operated an agency that has had its license suspended or revoked (especially if the agency has been sighted for failing to account for or disburse monies collected); and

    (d) If the agency is currently under investigation for any reason.*
4. Take the time to check references. Many collection agencies have impressive client lists, but they aren't always genuine. Also, there's no way of knowing what the clients on the list think of the agency's performance without taking the time to contact some of them. When checking references you should find out how responsive the agency has been to client inquiries, how frequently progress reports are issued, how long it takes the agency to remit the money it collects, and how often accounts are referred to outside counsel.
5. Beware of "money up front" schemes that require the collection agency user to pay a fee before any money has been collected. Most collection agencies work on a contingent basis, meaning the collection agency doesn't earn a fee until and unless it actually collects the client's money. Collection agencies that earn money only if they collect your accounts are bound to be more motivated than collection agencies that earn money whether they collect your accounts or not. The more motivated an agency is, the more money it is likely to recover for you.
6. Ask prospective collection agencies when you will receive your money, if and when the agency collects it. This is very important because the main purpose of a collection agency is to collect the client's money and return it as quickly as possible. You should select an agency that remits promptly on receipt. If money is collected by certified check, money order, bank wire transfer or in cash, it should be remitted to you immediately. If payment is in the form of a local company check or personal check (a check drawn on a bank located in the same city where the agency deposits the money), it should be remitted within five to seven working days. If payment is collected in the form of an out of town company check or personal check, it should be remitted within ten to fourteen working days.

---

*Don't let your guard down just because an agency has a clean bill of health from the collection agency licensing authorities in your state. For the most part enforcement of state collection agency statutes is very lax. Remember that it is your obligation to protect yourself from unscrupulous agencies.

Agencies that remit on a periodic basis are less desirable because their clients don't receive their money as quickly. Collection agencies that remit on a monthly schedule wait until the end of the month before disbursing the monies collected during the month. This is true even of guaranteed funds like certified checks, money orders, bank wire transfers, and cash. Wouldn't you rather have your money in your bank account than in the agency's bank account?

7. Learn all you can about the collection methods used by the collection agency. Is the agency providing only a letter-writing service? Does the agency rely on telephone contact? If so, does the agency have a WATS line to provide proper telephone follow-up? You should also determine if there are circumstances when the agency would arrange to collect your accounts in person. It's important to select an agency that is capable of adapting its collection approach to fit each situation. What works with one delinquent customer might not work with another. You should make sure the collection agency will give your accounts the attention they deserve. To do that, the agency must be capable of maintaining regular contact with each past-due customer from the time you place the account until it is resolved (either by collection or a determination that collection is not possible).

8. Look for a full-service collection agency with nationwide coverage (or worldwide coverage if you have international accounts). Some agencies are unable or unwilling to collect in all areas of the country. Instead of telling you that, however, many agencies will simply forward your accounts to other agencies located near the past-due customers. This defeats the purpose of getting to know the agency you originally placed your account with. Avoid agencies that delegate control of your accounts to affiliated agencies.

9. Ask the collection agency how it intends to advise you of the status of your accounts. Will you receive regular progress reports? How often? Will such reports be written or oral? If the reports are to be written, will individual reports be provided on each of your accounts as developments occur, or will mass reports covering all of your accounts be issued on a periodic basis? What will the reports tell you? Will they provide substantive information or sketchy information? The object is to select an agency that is capable of providing the kind of information you want, when you want it.

10. Check out the collection agency's policy on the withdrawal of accounts. Ask what you have to do to get your accounts back before you place them. You have an absolute right to the return of your accounts if you decide to withdraw them. There may, however, be strings attached to the release of some of your accounts.* This could happen if:
    (a) The delinquent customer is paying his or her account in regular installments.
    (b) The past-due customer has promised to pay his or her account by a specific date in the future.
    (c) The account is in the hands of an attorney who has actually spent time working on it.
    (d) Suit has been filed.
    (e) The agency has incurred extraordinary expenses (in locating or personally confronting a delinquent customer, for example).

PROTECTING YOURSELF FROM UNSCRUPULOUS AGENCIES

What if you have trouble with the collection agency you're using? What if you discover that payments made to the agency have not been remitted to you? What if the agency has used questionable, unethical, or illegal collection tactics? What if you just don't think the agency is doing a good job? Remember Wolner's Rule: *Marriage and collection agencies are both a lot easier to get into than to get out of.* Unfortunately, nearly all the statutes that govern the activities of collection agencies are designed to protect the people collection agencies collect *from*, not the people collection agencies collect *for*. If you become disenchanted with a collection agency and want your accounts returned, you should (1) immediately write a certified letter (with return receipt requested) to the agency requesting the return of your accounts, and (2) then notify the

---

*Collection agencies have an ever-increasing investment in the accounts you place with them. With rare exceptions, collection agency users who attempt to prevent agencies from earning fees by prematurely withdrawing their accounts will be charged full fees.

collection agency licensing authority in your state of your request for withdrawal.*

Smart credit granters protect themselves from the hassles of withdrawing accounts by entering into specific written agreements with the collection agencies they use, before they ever place their accounts. Here are my recommendations:

1. Give the collection agency a limited amount of time to work your accounts (three to six months should be sufficient). Insist that the agency close and return all accounts that have not been collected or referred to legal counsel within the time limit, unless you specifically authorize the agency to continue its efforts.
2. Determine the ground rules governing the release of accounts that the collection agency has referred to legal counsel with your permission. Much will depend on whether you have been responsible for advancing legal fees or whether the legal fees have been advanced by the agency or attorney. If you end up having to compensate an attorney to win the release of your accounts, make it clear that you'll need an itemization of the time the attorney has spent on each account and a full report describing exactly what the attorney did.
3. Insist on the immediate return of your accounts if the agency is shown to have acted improperly, unethically, or illegally.

Whether or not you suspect the collection agency you're using of unethical or illegal activities, it's a good idea to take a few precautions. Here are a few suggestions:

1. Contact customers you have previously placed with the agency in question. Find out how the collection agency handled these accounts. While the information you receive may not be completely objective, you'll have reason for concern if you hear similar complaints from a number of different customers.

---

*What happens next depends on state and local statutes. Collection agencies are usually given a specific number of days (thirty days is customary) to wrap up their collection efforts. You will be required to pay full fees on accounts collected during that period of time.

2. Periodically verify the balances of accounts you have placed with collection agencies by mailing balance confirmation notices to the affected customers. See figure 19. If balance discrepancies turn up between your records and the confirmations submitted by these customers, check them out. If there is a substantial discrepancy or the customer claims to have paid more than thirty days ago, ask for a copy of the front and back of the customer's cancelled check. If the agency did cash the check, call the agency and ask for a status report. If the agency fails to report the payment or denies receiving it, demand the immediate return of all your accounts and a full accounting of all the money the agency has collected on your behalf. Then contact the appropriate state regulatory authorities.
3. Maintain contact with the collection agency enforcement authorities in your state to determine if the agencies you're using are still licensed, have been suspended, or are being investigated for possible disciplinary action.
4. Visit the principal office of the collection agencies you select. It's best to do so unannounced. Ask to see specific accounts and request detailed explanations of the notations on the account cards.

THE COST

Collection fees normally are contingent on the actual recovery of money for a client. In addition, fees may vary depending on the size of the accounts involved. A fee of twenty-five percent of the amount collected is typical for nonlegal, commercial accounts of average size ($500 – $5,000). A fee of forty percent of the amount collected is typical for nonlegal, retail accounts ($100 and up). A fee of thirty-five percent of the amount collected is typical for legal, commercial accounts. A fee of fifty percent of the amount collected is typical for legal, retail accounts.*

Sometimes the attorneys retained by collection agencies on your behalf request a portion of their legal fees in advance on a noncontingent basis. These are known as "advance suit fees." An

---

*Collection agencies seldom forward accounts totaling less than $500 to legal counsel.

FIGURE 19
BALANCE CONFIRMATION LETTER

DAN A. WOLNER, PUBLISHER　　　Phone: 612-888-2252

October 14, 19 -

Mr. Steve Moll
COMPUTE-IT SERVICES CORPORATION
129 Disk Drive
Sofware, Minnesota 00000

Mr. Moll:　　　REQUEST FOR BALANCE CONFIRMATION

According to our records, the balance on your account #9999 as of August 30, 19 -, was $295.45.

If this amount does not agree with your records, please complete and return the form at the bottom of this letter. A postage-paid business reply envelope has been enclosed for your convenience.

Thank you,

Dan A. Wolner

Enclosure

Our records indicate an amount outstanding on August 30, 19 - of
$ _____.

Date and amount of last payment _____

Your name (please print or type) _____
Phone number (____)_____

P.O. Box 39657, Edina, MN 55439-0657

advance suit fee totaling ten percent of the account balance would not be unusual. If the suit is successful, the client would be charged the collection agency's normal legal rate less the amount of any suit fees advanced to the attorney. If the suit is unsuccessful, the client would forfeit the suit fees advanced to the attorney.

Collection fees are fairly standard throughout the collection industry. If you are approached by an agency that offers substantially lower fees than the rest, proceed with caution. A cut-rate agency is no bargain if it provides second-rate service.

GUIDELINES FOR COLLECTION AGENCY USERS

1. Provide the agency with as much information about your accounts as possible. Itemized statements, invoices, credit applications, and copies of letters sent to or received from delinquent customers are always helpful.
2. Require the agency to promptly acknowledge the accounts you place.
3. Check with the agency before cashing checks you receive directly from customers who have been placed for collection.
4. Notify the agency if you permit customers who have been placed for collection to return merchandise in lieu of payment. A fee will be due.
5. Make sure the agency receives your written authorization before threatening suit or forwarding your accounts to an attorney.
6. Ask the agency to provide you with copies of correspondence sent to or received from attorneys to whom your accounts have been forwarded.
7. Use an agency with a demonstrated knowledge of the legal process. The agency you select must be capable of closely monitoring the activities of attorneys retained on your behalf.
8. Don't allow an agency to settle accounts for less than the balance due without your written permission.
9. Don't discuss problem accounts with customers after their accounts have been placed with a collection agency. Refer all inquiries to the agency.
10. Don't send accounts to an agency unless you're sure they are due. Most agencies charge a fee if they discover that an account was paid before placement. You could be in for legal difficulties as well.

11. Don't place disputed accounts with an agency unless you notify the agency of the dispute when you place the accounts.
12. Don't allow the agency to accept extended payment arrangements (calling for payment of the balance due in more than thirty days) without your written permission.
13. Don't send accounts to a collection agency that have previously been placed with another agency unless the first agency discontinues its efforts and you advise the new agency that the accounts were worked by another agency.
14. Don't use agencies that allow collectors to conceal their identities by using aliases.

ADDITIONAL PROTECTION

An additional measure of security may be obtained by dealing with collection agencies that belong to any one of a number of professional associations. Commercial credit granters should take note that members of the Commercial Law League of America (CLLA), Commercial Collection Agency Section, New Providence, New Jersey, are required to carry a $50,000 surety bond and must comply with strict standards of ethical conduct and financial responsibility. This is particularly important since surety bonds are not mandated in every state, and those that do require them usually offer much less protection.

CHAPTER 16
COLLECTION ATTORNEYS

After doing everything possible to collect past-due accounts on your own, you may decide to turn them over to an attorney. Some credit granters feel delinquent customers are more likely to respond to attorneys. This decision is usually made when the amount owed exceeds the small claims court limit, or the credit granter believes attorney involvement will induce the delinquent customer to pay. Sometimes credit granters use collection attorneys when the amount owed is extremely large. They would rather gamble on an attorney being able to resolve the account quickly than commit themselves to paying a large collection agency fee. If you decide to turn your delinquent customers over to a collection attorney, you must:

1. Check out the attorney's credentials as a lawyer and as a collector. First, make sure the attorney is licensed to practice law in the jurisdiction where suit will be brought by contacting the state or local bar association in that jurisdiction. Then ask for the names and phone numbers of clients the attorney has collected money for in the past and take the time to call some of them.
2. Determine what the attorney will do and how he or she will do it. For example, if you have hired the attorney just to write collection letters, ask for sample copies of the letters to be used. If you have retained the attorney only to file suit, get a step-by-step explanation of what will be done and when it will be done.
3. Put your agreement with the attorney in writing. Then thoroughly read the agreement before you sign. In fact, it's probably a good idea to take a copy of the agreement home to read at your leisure. If you're unsure about anything, ask questions before signing. Make sure the agreement includes language:
(a) Covering the duties you expect the attorney to perform.

(b) Establishing the overall fee structure and placing a ceiling on the fee the attorney will be charging to collect each account. For example, if the attorney is charging on a contingent basis, find out what the rate will be and determine exactly what fees, if any, you will be responsible for advancing. If the attorney is charging by the hour, you should nail down the hourly rate and place a ceiling on the fee the attorney will be able to charge on each account without your permission. For example, instruct the attorney to suspend action and check with you before incurring fees in excess of fifty percent of the value of the account being handled. If the account is valued at $2,500, have the attorney contact you before fees reach $1,250.
(c) Asking for a monthly, bimonthly, or quarterly accounting of time spent and fees incurred. Never allow an attorney to operate carte blanche.
(d) Requesting periodic progress reports. It's best to ask the attorney to provide progress reports on a regular schedule (monthly, bimonthly, or quarterly). You have a right to know the status of your accounts.

THE COLLECTION ATTORNEY'S ROLE

Credit granters must clearly define the role they expect a collection attorney to play. Collection attorneys aren't always hired to collect money or file lawsuits. Some credit granters simply want to use the attorney's name to scare their past-due customers into paying. They expect the attorney to write a letter or two and that's it. If this is the role you want an attorney to play, there are a few things you should know about attorney letters. First, attorneys are not permitted to allow correspondence bearing their signatures (or facsimiles thereof) to be mailed by persons who are not in their exclusive employ. Second, attorneys cannot suggest or threaten actions that they do not intend to take.

Other credit granters expect collection attorneys to perform services identical to those performed by collection agencies. These collection attorneys correspond with delinquent customers, locate people who "skip out" on their debts, negotiate payment plans, and file lawsuits when necessary. Credit granters should seek contingent fee arrangements (fees contingent on the recovery of money) from attorneys who provide services similar to those offered by collection agencies. If that is not possible you're probably better off using a collection agency.

Still other credit granters place accounts with collection attorneys only when they want to sue someone. They're interested only in the attorney's technical ability to file lawsuits, obtain judgments, and attach assets.

Remember that before selecting a collection attorney it's important to decide exactly what you want the attorney to do. Once you have done that, it's time to find out whether the attorney will be able to do what you want him or her to do.

THE COST

Most attorneys charge by the hour. It is possible that a collection attorney will be successful in collecting an account by sending a couple of letters or making a few telephone calls. On the other hand, you may wind up paying for many hours of work (at fifty to two hundred dollars per hour) without recovering a cent. Unfortunately, there is no way of telling how much time an attorney will have to spend to collect a given account, so you should be very selective about the accounts you turn over to collection attorneys.

DISSATISFACTION WITH ATTORNEY

There are specific steps you should take if you are dissatisfied with the attorney you select:

1. Talk to the attorney by telephone or write the attorney a letter expressing why you are dissatisfied.
2. Ask for an explanation of the attorney's actions and the fees charged. Disputes between attorneys and clients generally revolve around fees. Give the attorney an opportunity to explain what he or she did and why. If fees are the primary problem and you're still dissatisfied after hearing the attorney's explanation, the attorney may voluntarily reduce his or her fee.
3. If you are unable to resolve your differences with the attorney and your dispute revolves around:
    (a) The attorney's fee—Contact your local attorney referral and information service or your state or local bar association about resolving your complaint through arbitration. Most

attorneys will arbitrate fee disputes.* To arbitrate a fee dispute both you and the attorney must agree to submit to arbitration. You will both be required to sign a form specifying that (1) you are dissatisfied with the fees charged, (2) you have made a good faith effort to resolve your differences with the attorney, and (3) you will agree to be bound by the decision of the fee arbitration panel. A hearing will then be held. The fee arbitration panel will gather evidence and hear testimony about the work the attorney performed and the fees charged. The panel will determine an equitable fee.

(b) The attorney's conduct—Attorneys may be dismissed at any time. If you discharge an attorney and retain a new attorney, your former attorney must return all files, documents, and papers belonging to you. The new attorney will then pick up where the other attorney left off. If you believe the former attorney's conduct has cost you money or harmed you in any material way, you may have grounds for a malpractice claim.** In that case, you should (1) assemble all evidence that backs up your claim, (2) seek the advice of another attorney, and (3) consult with the new attorney to determine if there is a reasonable belief that malpractice occurred.

ADDITIONAL POINTS

Legal action should not be authorized unless you have been assured by the attorney that the company or person being sued has attachable assets. Assets should be located before suit is filed.

It is essential for credit granters to have confidence in an attorney's ability to guide a case through the legal process. But it's

---

*If you are not able to come to terms with your attorney on an equitable fee, submit your complaint to arbitration immediately. Don't wait for your attorney to initiate proceedings against you to recover fees. At that point, arbitration will not be possible.

**If you suspect legal malpractice, seek legal advice immediately. Legal malpractice cases are governed by a statute of limitations (ordinarily six years). Your claim will be barred if you delay action beyond the statute of limitations.

Collection Attorneys 161

just as important to find a collection attorney who will counsel you against filing suit when your chance of recovery is slim.

It's not easy to find collection attorneys. While there are lots of attorneys, not all of them are capable of collecting money. In addition, many attorneys are unwilling to handle collection accounts unless they are very large or you are likely to place a number of accounts with them.

Remember that you must find an attorney who is licensed to practice in the jurisdiction where suit is to be filed. This could be a problem if the company or person you're suing is in another city or state.

CHAPTER 17
ALTERNATIVE DISPUTE RESOLUTION

This chapter concludes the discussion of alternative collection measures. It was specifically written to advise credit granters of non-adversarial dispute resolution processes known as *alternative dispute resolution,* or simply ADR. Typically we think of mediation and arbitration as the primary ADR methods. For too long, credit granters have been under the impression that there are only two ways to respond to collection problems: doing nothing or reacting aggressively. Fearing the loss of business that might result from an aggressive approach to collections, many credit granters have opted to do nothing. Unfortunately, these credit granters have overlooked a viable alternative to confrontational collection procedures. ADR allows credit granters to resolve mutual problems and preserve—even strengthen—business relationships.

WHAT IS MEDIATION?

Mediation is a process that:

1. Is completely voluntary. All parties to the dispute must agree to submit to mediation.
2. Allows the conflicting parties to fully explore the issues dividing them.
3. Is designed to achieve workable solutions that all the parties will be able to support.
4. Does not impose solutions on the parties but provides a framework within which the parties may negotiate and reach their own solutions.

WHEN MEDIATION SHOULD BE USED

If you're typical of other people who have been exposed to the concept of mediation for the first time, you're probably skeptical that a totally voluntary process will work. After all, most credit granters feel they have already given their delinquent customers plenty of time and every opportunity to come to terms. But mediation works precisely because it is a voluntary process. There is usually a high degree of commitment to mediated agreements because the parties have chosen to negotiate instead of being forced to negotiate.

Of course, mediation doesn't work in every situation. The following tips will help you determine when mediation might be effective in resolving a dispute:

1. The parties must be highly involved and the issues clearly defined. There should be a sense of urgency to resolve the conflict.
2. The parties must enter the negotiations with an equal stake in the outcome. Both stand to gain if the problem is resolved, and both stand to lose if it isn't.
3. The parties must be willing to compromise to reach an agreement.
4. The parties must assure each other that once an agreement is reached, it will be implemented.
5. The parties must believe that the mediator is impartial and interested only in helping the parties resolve their differences.

STRUCTURING THE MEDIATION PROCESS

Credit granters and their delinquent customers get bogged down in their problems just like other disputants. Mediation appeals to the feeling in all of us that it's better to go the extra mile in an effort to rise above differences than it is to succumb to feelings of bitterness, hostility, pettiness, and suspicion.

The mediation process must be carefully structured to succeed. It consists of five distinct phases:

1. Renewing the commitment to mediation—Before the parties can be brought together, they must express their willingness to submit their dispute to mediation. When negotiations begin the parties must recommit themselves to the mediation process. In

addition, the mediator must make it clear that he or she has confidence in the ability of the disputants to resolve their differences.
2. Establishing the ground rules—It must be understood that the mediator's role is to facilitate communication between the parties, not to propose or impose solutions on them. The parties should be encouraged to vent their feelings constructively, by focusing on the problems, not on the people.
3. Defining the problem:
    (a) Each party should be interviewed separately before mediation begins.
    (b) The mediator must differentiate between real and imagined problems and risks.
    (c) The mediator must identify issues that can and cannot be changed.
    (d) The mediator must clarify the positions of the parties and legitimize their perceptions.
    (e) The mediator should encourage the free flow of ideas and stimulate discussion by asking "what if . . . " questions. This allows the parties to explore hypothetical solutions to their problems without committing themselves to a particular proposal.
    (f) The mediator must assist the parties in reaching a consensus on the facts of the case.
4. Solving the problem—The mediator should:
    (a) Focus on the natural inclination toward fairness.
    (b) Suggest a range of options and explore the likely consequences of each option.
    (c) Obtain commitments on a list of options.
    (d) Narrow down the list of options.
5. Reaching an agreement:
    (a) Define the terms of the potential agreement.
    (b) If an agreement is reached, it should be written up and signed by the parties. A copy of the agreement should then be given to each party. A mediated agreement generally is not binding unless it contains a clause that states that it is binding and a clause that states that the parties have been advised in writing that (1) the mediator has no duty to protect their interests or give them information about their legal rights; (2) their signing of such an agreement may

adversely affect their legal rights; and (3) they should consult an attorney before signing such an agreement if they are uncertain about their rights.*

(c) Regardless of whether an agreement is reached or not, the parties should be commended for their efforts in attempting to reach an agreement.

(d) If an agreement is not reached, the parties should be encouraged to contact the mediator for assistance as it is needed. This will keep the channels of communication open.

COLLECTING MONEY

Credit granters have informally mediated collection disputes for many years, usually when a particular collection problem threatened to destroy an ongoing relationship with a high-volume customer. Often, however, the credit granter was put in the unenviable position of taking a firm stand and losing the customer's business, or capitulating and keeping it. With other suppliers eagerly waiting to serve these high-volume customers, the affected credit granters had little choice. The relative disparity of power made it difficult for the parties to mediate on an equal footing. When it comes to dealing with medium- to low-volume customers, however, credit granters are in a much stronger position. These customers are likely to need their suppliers just as much as their suppliers need them. As mentioned earlier in this chapter, mediation is more effective when all parties have an equal stake in the outcome.

Unfortunately, few companies are aware that community mediation services exist. Fewer still are aware that mediation provides credit granters with an alternative form of dispute resolution that is often cheaper, less time-consuming, and more conducive to maintaining business relationships than suing. Mediation holds great promise for credit granters—particularly small business credit granters—who want to protect their customer base and avoid the expense, time loss, and ill will that accompanies

---

*Points one through three are based on sections 595.02 and 572.31 through 572.40 of the Minnesota Statutes. For information about the mediation statutes in your jurisdiction, contact your local or state bar association.

adversarial collection measures. For mediation to become effective in resolving collection problems (or other business problems for that matter), people will have to learn more about the concept of nonjudicial dispute resolution and serve as catalysts to promote the use of mediation to resolve disputes.

FINDING A COMPETENT MEDIATOR

The mediation process is usually governed by statute. In most jurisdictions a mediator must provide parties who have expressed their desire to mediate a dispute with a written statement of qualifications before mediation begins. The written statement of qualifications should describe the mediator's educational background and relevant training and experience in the field. Ask questions and thoroughly investigate the background of any person who represents himself or herself as a mediator. If you need help in locating a competent mediator or are interested in learning more about mediation in general, call or write your state or local bar association.

ARBITRATION

Arbitration is a process by which conflicting parties agree to submit their dispute to an impartial third party who will consider the facts of the case and render a decision. There are two types of arbitration decisions, non-binding and binding. A non-binding decision is advisory only. The parties may decide to accept or reject it. On the other hand, binding decisions result when the parties agree in writing to be bound by the decision of the arbitrator. For the purpose of this chapter, when the term binding arbitration is used it refers to pre-dispute arbitration, or agreement to submit future disputes to arbitration. The agreement may be contained in a separate document, or incorporated into a credit application or sales contract. Figure 2B contains an example of a credit application containing a pre-arbitration agreement. Either party may request submission of a dispute to an arbitrator. When a decision has been reached, the arbitrator's "award" may be confirmed by the court, at which time it will become a legally enforceable judgment.

NACM ADR PROGRAM

The National Association of Credit Management (NACM) has entered into an agreement with Equilaw Incorporated, Minneapolis, MN, which provides NACM members who have signed arbitration agreements on file with access to the services of Equilaw's National Arbitration Forum (NAF). The process would begin when such an NACM member advises his NACM affiliate that the provisions of a valid ADR agreement are being enforced.

The NACM affiliate will assist the member in filling out the appropriate forms. A nominal fee will be charged by the affiliate for processing. A separate filing fee, based on the amount of the claim and payable to NAF must be submitted with the completed paperwork. The NACM affiliate will forward the filing fee and the appropriate copies of the claim to NAF in Minneapolis, MN. At the request of the claimant, the filing fee may be added to any award the claimant receives.

NAF will examine the paperwork and determine if the claim is properly documented. If the claim is totally without merit, NAF will return the claim and the filing fee to the NACM affiliate. If the claim appears valid, NAF will open a file and assign a case number. If the claim is poorly documented, NAF may request additional information. Once satisfied with the authenticity of the claim, NAF will retain one copy and return two receipted copies to the claimant. The claimant is responsible for effecting service of process according to the Federal Rules of Civil Procedure. NAF will take no further action until the "respondent" has been served. If service cannot be effected NAF will issue a partial refund. If service is effected, the respondent must reply to the claimant in writing (with a copy to NAF) within 30 days. If there is no reply an administrative hearing will be held, at which time a default award may be granted to the claimant.

HEARINGS

If the respondent does reply, but merely presents an explanation instead of a defense, a document hearing will be held. Hearings are conducted by qualified arbitrators who are bound by the NAF code of ethics. All document hearings are held at the Minneapolis office of NAF. Document hearings consist of a review of the evidence submitted by the claimant and respondent. The respondent may choose to mount a defense and file a counterclaim. To file a counterclaim, the respondent must pay the appropriate filing fee and provide NAF with appropriate evidence. The parties may ask each other to produce certain information, and may ask for subpoenas to compel the release of such information from each other, or from third persons.

Either party may request a participatory hearing within ten days after the date specified on the notice of a document hearing. This request must be in writing and accompanied by an additional fee. The parties are notified of the participatory hearing date at least 15 days in advance. Participatory hearings usually take place within 12 weeks, and are similar to a trial. Witnesses may be called, testimony taken, and exhibits entered by the parties themselves or their representatives.

By entering into a pre-dispute binding arbitration agreement, the NACM ADR program provides credit granters with a unique mechanism to assure customers that future disputes will not end up in court. While the fees are significant (contact your local NACM affiliate, or Equilaw Incorporated, Minneapolis, MN, for an NAF fee schedule) the process is specifically designed to control costs, promote continuing relationships, and reach quick, enforceable solutions that are mutually beneficial to all concerned.

CONCLUSION

Now that you have finished this book, it's time to apply what you have learned. First, you must get to know your customers by finding and analyzing information that will tell you the level of risk you are exposed to. Next, you must use the information you have gathered to make an intelligent credit-granting decision. Then you must systematically follow up to detect, confront, and resolve problem accounts. Last, you must know what to do and what not to do when your usual collection efforts have failed to produce results.

By explaining the benefits of effective credit management, enhancing the interpersonal skills of credit-granting and debt collecting personnel, and expanding the knowledge of credit granters, this book will pay for itself many times in the future. Remember, however, that every company is different and what works for one may not work for another.

While this book does not claim to have all the answers, it may help you avoid a catastrophic credit-granting mistake or recover money you thought was lost. If so, I would be delighted. Frankly, however, it would please me just as much to know that the book has given you one or two fewer things to worry about when you go to bed at night.

APPENDIX A
READABILITY INDEX

Many people clutter their letters with complex words and sentences. When it comes to writing letters, simplicity is the watchword. The following formula will help you check your letters for reading ease. It will also assist you in changing your writing style to make your letters more effective. To find the readability index:

1. Pick a passage from one of your letters that is at least 100 words long.
2. Find the average number of words in each sentence by dividing the number of words in the passage by the number of sentences in the passage. Independent clauses joined by a comma or semicolon should be treated as separate sentences if a period could replace the comma or semicolon.
3. Count the number of words in the passage containing three or more syllables.
4. Add the average number of words per sentence and the number of three or more syllable words together and multiply the result by 0.4.

$$\begin{pmatrix} \text{Average number} \\ \text{of words per} \\ \text{sentence} \end{pmatrix} + \begin{pmatrix} \text{Number of 3 or more} \\ \text{syllable words} \end{pmatrix} \times 0.4 = \text{Readability index}$$

The readability index is roughly equivalent to school grade reading ability. For example, if the readability index of one of your collection letters is twelve, someone with the reading ability generally associated with a high school graduate should find it easy to read the letter.

The ideal readability index for a collection letter depends on the reading ability of the person you are writing to. Everyone is different. However, since there is no way to determine the reading ability of the people you write to, you should keep your letters simple. I recommend a readability index of 9 to 12.

APPENDIX B
EQUAL CREDIT OPPORTUNITY ACT

The federal Equal Credit Opportunity Act prohibits discrimination against credit applicants on the basis of sex, marital status, race, color, religion, national origin, age, and other factors. This explanation of the act deals specifically with the provisions that apply to sex, marital status, and age.

The Equal Credit Opportunity Act does not give anyone an automatic right to credit. It does require credit granters to uniformly apply creditworthiness standards to all credit applicants.

CREDITWORTHINESS

Creditors choose various criteria to rate the credit risk posed by each potential credit customer. Creditors may ask about finances (the amount of money earned, the kinds of savings and investments held, and the sources of additional income, for example). They may look for signs of reliability (the applicant's occupation, the length of time the applicant has been employed, the length of time the applicant has lived at the same address, and whether the applicant owns or rents his or her home, for example). They may also examine the applicant's credit record (how much the applicant owes, how often the applicant has borrowed, and how the applicant has managed past debts, for example). Creditors want to be assured of two things: the applicant's ability to repay debt and the applicant's willingness to do so. The Equal Credit Opportunity Act does not change this standard of creditworthiness.

EQUAL CREDIT OPPORTUNITY

The law says that a creditor may not discriminate against a credit applicant—treat one applicant less favorably than another applicant—on the basis of sex, marital status, or age. The mere fact that a credit applicant is male or female, unmarried (includes single, divorced, and widowed) or married, young (as long as the person is of legal age) or old, is not by itself sufficient reason to turn down a credit application. The following rules are designed to stop specific abuses that have limited the ability of people to get credit.

QUESTIONS ABOUT AN APPLICANT'S SEX, MARITAL STATUS, OR AGE

A creditor may not discourage an applicant from applying for credit on the basis of sex, marital status, or age. Creditors and applicants should be aware that there are very specific rules governing the kinds of questions applicants may be asked about their sex, marital status, or age:

1. Credit applicants may not be asked their sex on a credit application—with one exception. If an applicant applies for a loan to buy or build a home, a creditor is required to ask the applicant to provide the federal government with information to monitor compliance with the act. However, applicants are not required to answer.
2. Applicants do not have to choose a courtesy title (Mr., Miss, Ms., Mrs.) on a credit form.
3. A creditor may not request an applicant's marital status on an application for an individual, unsecured account, unless the applicant lives in a community property state or relies on property located in a community property state to support the application.
4. A creditor may request an applicant's marital status in all other cases, but the applicant can only be asked whether he or she is married, unmarried (includes single, divorced, widowed), or separated.
5. A creditor may ask how old a credit applicant is. However, the use of this information is restricted. The law says that an applicant's age may not be the basis for an arbitrary decision to deny or decrease credit if the applicant would otherwise qualify. An applicant may not be turned down for credit just because he or she is over a certain age.

RATING CREDIT APPLICANTS AS A CREDIT RISK

To make sure that all applicants are treated fairly, there are certain other things creditors may not do when deciding whether applicants are creditworthy.

1. Specifically, with respect to sex or marital status, a creditor may not:
   (a) Refuse to consider an applicant's income because he or she is married, even if the applicant's income is from part-time employment.
   (b) Ask the applicant about birth control practices or plans to have children. In addition, a creditor may not assume that a credit applicant will have children or that income will be interrupted by having children.
   (c) Refuse to consider reliable alimony, child support, or separate maintenance payments. However, an applicant receiving such income is not required to disclose its existence unless he or she chooses to do so voluntarily to improve the chances of getting credit.
   (d) Consider whether the applicant has a telephone listing in his or her own name.
   (e) Consider the applicant's sex as a factor in deciding whether he or she is a good credit risk.
   (f) Use the applicant's marital status to discriminate against him or her. However, there are some closely related questions that are permitted. To estimate an applicant's expenses, a creditor may ask how many children the person has, their ages, and the cost of caring for them, as well as the applicant's obligation to make alimony, child support, or separate maintenance payments. A creditor may ask how regularly the applicant receives alimony, child support, or separate maintenance payments and whether such payments are made under court order to determine whether these payments represent a dependable source of income. The applicant may also be asked whether there is a telephone in his or her home. Finally, a creditor may consider the applicant's marital status if, under the laws of the state, there are differences in the property rights of married and unmarried people. Such differences may affect a creditor's ability to collect in the event of default.
2. With respect to age, a creditor may not:
   (a) Refuse to consider an applicant's retirement income in rating his or her credit application.
   (b) Require a person with an existing credit account to reapply, change the terms of the account, or close the account just because a person reaches a certain age or retires.

(c) Deny credit to an applicant or close an existing credit account because credit life insurance or other credit-related insurance is not available to persons in that age category. Of course, age does have economic consequences. The earnings of young applicants just entering the work force are likely to grow over the years. But a young applicant's expenses are probably rising too, and a young person may not have much of a credit record to rely on. A person nearing retirement age is likely to face the loss of income over the next few years. But the expenses of a person approaching retirement age are probably decreasing too, and an elderly person may have a solid credit history to support his or her credit application. All of this information could have an important effect on an applicant's creditworthiness, but not all of it will show up on a credit application. The law therefore permits a creditor to consider information related to age that has a clear bearing on a person's ability and willingness to repay the debt. Consider the following example: Jones applies for a mortgage loan for thirty years with a five percent down payment. Jones is sixty-three years old, and his income will be reduced when he retires in two years. The loan is denied. Jones might meet the bank's standards if the down payment were larger, if the loan had a shorter term with higher monthly payments, or if savings and investments—or other assets easily converted into cash—could be offered as security for the loan.

EXTENDING CREDIT—OPENING AND MAINTAINING INDIVIDUAL ACCOUNTS

The law says that every person has a right to credit if he or she is creditworthy. Therefore, a creditor may not:

1. Refuse to grant an applicant his or her own individual account because of sex, marital status, or age.
2. Refuse to open or maintain a separate account in the applicant's name alone (or in the applicant's maiden name).
3. Ask for information about an applicant's spouse or former spouse, unless:
   (a) The applicant is relying on spousal income.
   (b) The spouse intends to use the account and be liable for it.

(c) The applicant is relying on alimony, child support, or separate maintenance payments to support the application for credit.
(d) The applicant lives in a community property state or is relying on property located in a community property state to support application for credit.
4. Require a cosigner or the signature of the applicant's spouse just because the person is married (with certain exceptions when property rights are involved).

If a person's marital status changes, a creditor may not require the person with an existing credit account to reapply, change the terms of the account, or close the account, unless there is some indication that the person who will be responsible for the account is unable or unwilling to repay debts incurred. A creditor may ask an applicant to reapply if the original decision to extend credit was wholly or partially based on spousal earnings.

ESTABLISHING A CREDIT HISTORY

Some credit applicants (particularly married women) have trouble establishing credit histories because their credit transactions are listed under the name of their spouse. A new rule helps such applicants build up credit records of their own. The rule applies to information that creditors furnish to credit bureaus and other creditors about any account used by both husband and wife or on which both husband and wife are liable. Such information must be reported in both the name of the husband and of the wife.

The law also provides new guidelines for considering credit histories. If a credit history is used in the rating of a credit application, creditors must:

1. Consider the available credit history on all accounts the applicant holds or has previously held jointly with the spouse.
2. Consider all information that supports the applicant's contention that a favorable credit history on any account maintained in the name of the applicant's spouse accurately reflects the applicant's credit history.

Sometimes people who were but are no longer married have trouble getting credit because the applicant's former spouse was a poor credit risk. The law also says that a creditor must consider all information that supports the applicant's contention that an unfavorable credit history on any account shared with the applicant's spouse does not accurately reflect the applicant's credit history.

Another federal law, the Fair Credit Reporting Act, gives applicants the right to get a summary of their credit histories from credit reporting agencies and to correct inaccurate information in them.

NOTICE AND PENALTIES

Creditors may not drag their feet in processing credit applications. Applicants must be notified within thirty days of any action taken on a credit application. If credit is denied, the notice must be in writing and must either give specific reasons for the denial or tell the applicant that he or she is entitled to request such an explanation. Persons whose existing credit accounts have been closed have a right to the same notification.

If an applicant is denied credit, he or she is entitled to know why. If the creditor does not provide an explanation as provided by law, a credit applicant has a right under the Equal Credit Opportunity Act to sue for actual damages, plus a penalty if the violation was intentional. The court will also award reasonable attorneys' fees if a violation is actually proved.

THE MOST IMPORTANT RULES

1. An applicant cannot be refused credit just because he or she is male or female, unmarried (includes single, divorced, widowed) or married, young (as long as the person is of legal age) or old.
2. An applicant cannot be refused credit because a creditor assumes he or she will have children or that income will be interrupted by having children.
3. An applicant cannot be denied credit because a creditor refuses to consider regular payments for alimony, child support, or separate maintenance as income.
4. An applicant is entitled to have credit in his or her own name if he or she is creditworthy.
5. When an applicant applies for his or her own credit and relies on his or her own income, information about the applicant's spouse

or the cosignature of the spouse can be required only in certain circumstances.
6. Persons with existing credit accounts are entitled to keep their own accounts and their own credit histories regardless of changes in marital status.
7. Husbands and wives are able to build up their own independent credit records because all credit accounts must be carried in the names of both husband and wife, if both use the account or are liable for it.
8. If an applicant is denied credit, he or she has a right to find out why.

This explanation is not intended to be a complete or official summary of the Equal Credit Opportunity Act.

APPENDIX C
FAIR CREDIT REPORTING ACT

The Fair Credit Reporting Act was passed in 1971. The act provides legal protection of consumer privacy by:

1. Limiting the purposes for which a consumer credit report may be issued.
2. Giving consumers the opportunity to request full disclosure of the information in their own credit files.
3. Restricting the length of time adverse information may be retained in a credit file.
4. Letting consumers know when a credit report has contributed to a credit denial.
5. Allowing consumers to dispute the accuracy of information contained in their own credit files and to explain their side of the story.
6. Limiting access to credit files by governmental agencies.
7. Providing civil and criminal liability for violations of the act.

WHEN REPORTS MAY BE ISSUED

Credit reports may be issued in connection with the decision to extend credit, credit file updates, collection of accounts, employment applications, or other legitimate business reasons. To obtain access to credit files, credit granters must sign an agreement that certifies that reports will be requested only for legitimate purposes.

WHEN CREDIT IS DENIED ON THE BASIS OF A CREDIT REPORT

The Fair Credit Reporting Act provides that credit granters denying credit to a consumer must give the consumer the name and address of a credit bureau or other credit reporting service, if the information issued by that credit bureau or credit reporting service in any way contributed to the denial of credit. It is preferable to provide the consumer with this information in writing.

WHEN CREDIT BUREAU REPORTS CONTRIBUTE TO CREDIT DENIALS

Whenever a credit granter denies credit based on information from a source other than a credit bureau, such as a credit inquiry from another creditor, the consumer must be notified at the time of the credit denial that he or she has sixty days to make a written request for the nature of the information. Credit granters are not required to disclose, and should not disclose, the identity of any credit information source, unless the source has given explicit permission to do so. Credit granters are required to give the consumer enough information so that he or she may challenge the accuracy of the information.

LIMITATIONS ON ADVERSE INFORMATION

With the exception of a straight bankruptcy that may be reported for ten years, no adverse information may be included in a credit report that is more than seven years old. These limitations do not apply if the information is sought in connection with an application for credit or life insurance that totals more than $50,000, or when an employment report is for a job that pays a salary in excess of $20,000.

SPECIAL INVESTIGATIONS

An investigative credit report is one that contains information about an individual's character, reputation, or lifestyle, and that is obtained through personal interviews with friends, neighbors, relatives, or other third persons. Credit bureau reports do not contain such information. Reports that do contain such information are usually requested for insurance or employment purposes. If an employer orders an employment report that contains this type of information the applicant must be notified in writing, within three days after the report was ordered, that such a report has been requested and that it will include information about the applicant's character, reputation, or lifestyle. The applicant must also be advised of the employer's responsibility to disclose the nature and scope of the investigation within five days if the applicant requests it.

WHAT TYPE OF INFORMATION SHOULD A CREDIT GRANTER DISCLOSE?

Credit granters may furnish ledger experience about a consumer without having to comply with the stringent interviewing, notifying, correcting, and record keeping requirements that consumer credit reporting agencies are required to comply with, provided the information is accurate. But credit granters may fall under consumer credit reporting agency requirements if they provide anything other than factual ledger experience.

GOVERNMENT AGENCIES

The same requirements that apply to every credit granter's access to credit information also apply to government agencies. There must be a legitimate purpose for obtaining credit information from a credit bureau file (employment checks, collecting obligations owed to the government, and security clearances, for example). However, government agencies are able to obtain identification information, such as name, address, former addresses, and employment information, from credit bureau files. There may also be occasions when credit information will be disclosed in response to a court order. Consumers may direct the credit bureau to release confidential credit information from their own credit files to those requesting it.

This explanation is not intended to be a complete or official summary of the Fair Credit Reporting Act.

APPENDIX D
THE FAIR CREDIT BILLING ACT

The Fair Credit Billing Act, an addition to the Truth in Lending Act, requires creditors to promptly correct billing mistakes. The following explains how the act works to resolve billing disputes and protect a customer's credit rating.

BILLING ERRORS

Customers may challenge either the purchase or the price of an item that appears on a billing statement. The law defines an error as any charge:

1. Not made either by the customer or someone authorized to use the customer's account;
2. Poorly identified, for a different amount, or on a different date than is shown on the statement;
3. Something that the customer did not accept on delivery or which was not delivered according to agreement.

Billing errors also include:

1. Failure to credit a customer's account properly;
2. Computational or accounting mistakes;
3. Failure to mail a customer's statement to his or her current address, provided the creditor was notified of the address change at least ten days before the billing period ended.

A request for additional information or an explanation about a questionable item is also considered a billing error.

IN CASE OF ERROR

A creditor is required to take action to correct a billing error if the following steps are taken by a customer:

1. The customer notifies the creditor in writing within 60 days after the bill was mailed of:
   (a) His or her name and account number;
   (b) His or her belief that the bill contains an error and the specific reasons why he or she believes there is an error;
   (c) The suspected amount of the error.
2. While the customer is waiting for an answer, he or she does not have to pay the amount in question (the "disputed amount") or any minimum payments or finance charges that apply to it. But the customer is still obligated to pay all parts of the bill that are not in dispute.
3. The creditor must acknowledge a customer's billing error letter within thirty days, unless the bill is corrected before that. Within two billing periods—but in no case more than ninety days—the customer's account must either be corrected or the customer must be told why the creditor believes the bill is correct.
4. If the creditor made a mistake, the customer will not be required to pay any finance charges on the disputed amount. The customer's account must be corrected for either the full amount in dispute or for a part of that amount along with an explanation of what is still owed. The customer then has the time usually given on similar types of accounts to pay any balance. If no error is found, the creditor must promptly send the customer a statement of what is owed. In this case, the creditor may include any finance charges that accumulated and any minimum payments the customer missed while he or she was questioning the bill.
5. If the customer still isn't satisfied, he or she must notify the creditor within the time the customer has to pay the bill. However, the creditor has now fulfilled the legal obligation (except for the requirements that follow regarding the customer's credit rating).

CREDIT RATINGS

Once a customer has written about a possible error, the creditor may not give out information to other creditors or credit bureaus or threaten to damage the customer's credit rating. Until the customer's letter is answered, the creditor also may not take any collection action on the disputed amount or restrict the customer's account because of the dispute. A creditor can, however, apply the disputed amount against the customer's credit limit.

After the bill has been explained—and if the customer still disagrees in writing within the time allowed for payment and does not pay—the creditor can report the customer as delinquent on his or her account and begin collection proceedings. If this is done, the creditor must also report that the customer challenges the bill, and the customer must be provided in writing with the name and address of each person to whom such credit information has been given. When the matter is settled, the creditor must report the outcome to each person who received information about the customer's account.

DEFECTIVE MERCHANDISE OR SERVICES

The law provides that a customer may withhold payment of any balance due on defective merchandise or services purchased with a credit card, provided the customer has made a good faith effort to return the goods or resolve the problem with the merchant from whom the customer made the purchase. If the store that honored the credit card was not also the issuer of the card, two limitations apply to this right: (1) The original amount of the purchase must have exceeded $50; and (2) The sale must have taken place in the customer's state or within one hundred miles of the customer's current address. In the case of defective merchandise or services, the creditor may have to take legal action to determine the validity of the customer's claim.

PENALTIES AND OTHER PROVISIONS

The law provides that any creditor who fails to comply with these rules applying to billing errors and credit ratings automatically forfeits the amount of the item in question and any finance charges on it, up to a total of $50, even if no error occurred. Customers may also sue for actual damages plus twice the amount of any finance charges, in any case not less than $100 or more than $1,000. Class action suits are also permitted.

The law also includes requirements for prompt reporting and crediting of payments or return of merchandise. In addition, it provides that credit card issuers may not prohibit stores that honor their cards from offering discounts to customers who pay in cash or by check.

Creditors must provide customer's with a complete statement of their rights under the Fair Credit Billing Act when the account is first opened and at least twice annually (or send a shorter version with each billing).

This explanation is not intended to be a complete or official summary of the Fair Credit Billing Act.

APPENDIX E
SKIPTRACING GUIDE

People who "skip out" on their debts fall into two general categories:

1. Inadvertent skips. These people are well intentioned but careless. They don't make a conscious effort to avoid their creditors. It is relatively easy to locate them because they don't try to conceal their activities and whereabouts from friends, relatives, and employers.
2. Intentional skips. These people intentionally avoid their creditors. It is quite difficult to locate them because they do try to conceal their activities and whereabouts from friends, relatives, and employers. In fact, it is not unusual for these people to move frequently and to keep to themselves. There are three types of intentional skips:
   (a) Those who originally intended to pay but who find it impossible to pay because of personal problems, unemployment, money mismanagement, and so forth. These people often pay their creditors when conditions improve.
   (b) Those who never intended to pay and who purchase goods and services on credit for their own personal use. These people usually keep their purchases small to reduce the likelihood of credit granters pursuing them.
   (c) Those who never intended to pay and who illegally resell merchandise purchased on credit for cash. These people usually grab as much salable merchandise as they can lay their hands on without regard for the consequences.

TRAITS OF A GOOD SKIPTRACER

Skiptracers must project an image of warmth, friendliness, curiosity, and patience. The people you contact to find a skip must believe that you are sincere, that you have honorable intentions, and that you are committed to finding the skip no matter how much time and effort you have to expend. It is important not to tell the people you contact any more than is absolutely necessary. You should identify yourself and provide a telephone number and address where you may be reached. If pressed for a reason why you are calling, it's best to say only that you are calling about an important personal matter. You should not discuss the specifics of collection problems with anyone other than the person who actually owes the money. You should not use subterfuge to obtain information. You should never disclose false or misleading information (or any information you are unable to prove) to a third person that will harm the person you are trying to locate. Doing so could result in a lawsuit against you for slander (if the information was communicated verbally) or libel (if the information was communicated in writing).

You should never use intimidating tactics to locate a skip. It is a crime under both state and federal laws to use the telephone or the mails to threaten, abuse, or harass any person. Penalties for violations include fines, imprisonment, or both.

When attempting to locate a skip, it is important to get as much information as possible the first time you communicate with each person. Follow-up contacts are usually less productive than initial contacts because people often have second thoughts about the information they originally provided.

It is extremely important for skiptracers to keep accurate records of what they discover. The more information you are able to accumulate the easier it will be to locate the skip. Also, information gathered from one person is often helpful in extracting additional information from another person.

GETTING THE INFORMATION YOU NEED

Sometimes when skiptracing you will encounter third persons who are willing to talk freely. In this situation, you may be able to find out what you need to know by asking a question like, "Where is Charlie Jones living now, anyway?" At other times, you will encounter third persons who are more reluctant to talk. In such situations a more subtle approach may be more productive. For example, "I thought sure I had an address for Charlie Jones written down somewhere, but I can't seem to find it. Do you have it handy?"

SKIPTRACING RESOURCES

Skiptracers have many resources to choose from. There are four primary sources:

1. Public sources—Telephone company, directory assistance, post office, gas, electric, water, refuse services, tax assessor, state motor vehicle registration office, local licensing agencies, state incorporation and business registration offices.

    The first thing you should do is find out if the skip's telephone has been disconnected and if so, whether the telephone company has a referral number. If there is a referral number and the skip is a consumer, it's a good bet that the party to whom the calls are being referred is a relative or close friend. If the skip is a company, calls are often referred to the owner's home or to a new business venture operated by the owner of the company you are trying to locate.

    Directory assistance operators are also extremely helpful. If the skip has an unusual last name you may be able to locate relatives by asking the directory assistance operator for the telephone numbers of people with the same last name. You'll be able to get several numbers at one time for a nominal charge.

    Next, you should find out if the skip has left a forwarding address. To do that, write the word, "address correction requested" on the outside of the envelope of any letter you mail to the skip's previous address. If there is a forwarding address on file, the post office will send it to you for a nominal charge. Forwarding orders expire within one year so act quickly. If the debtor uses a post office box, you should call or write to the branch postmaster and request the registered name, phone number and address of the box holder.

    Gas, electric, water, refuse services, and the county tax assessor are all excellent resources to check. Contact the appropriate provider or tax office to verify the address being used for billing purposes. Express your concern about bills being sent to the correct address, then ask, "What address do you show in your system?"

If the skip is a consumer, the department of motor vehicles may have current location information. If the skip is a company, the department that regulates business licenses and corporations will have location information concerning the registered agent for service of process.

2. Commercial sources—City directories, consumer and commercial credit reporting agencies, newspapers.

    You may purchase city directories for your locality, but they're also available at most libraries. These directories cross-reference information by name, street address, and telephone number. Thus it is a simple matter to locate the skip's neighbors and people with the same or similar names. The skip's previous or present employer may also be listed.

    Credit reporting agencies may have information about the skip's creditors, bank, and employer. And newspapers are also a valuable source of information. Skips have babies, become engaged, marry, and get picked up for traffic violations. When they do, their names usually show up in the newspaper.

3. Credit applications—This is potentially your most productive source of leads. A credit application may give you the names of former and present employers, relatives, personal references, bank information, and trade references. Every bit of information listed in the skip's credit application will be of value in locating the skip.

4. Other sources—Trade Associations, competitors, NACM affiliates.

    Contact professional trade associations the debtor may have joined, or speak with companies in the same industry. Competitors often have a wealth of information and are ready, willing and able to talk. If the debtor is in an industry or profession that requires licensing or accreditation, contact the appropriate agency. NACM affiliates are another valuable resource. There are NACM offices located in major cities across the country staffed by dedicated credit professionals who are always ready to assist members.

APPENDIX F
THE FAIR DEBT COLLECTION PRACTICES ACT

The Fair Debt Collection Practices Act took effect on March 20, 1978. It is one of a series of laws enacted by Congress in recent years to protect consumers in credit transactions. This law is intended to stop abusive practices engaged in by some debt collectors.

THE SCOPE OF THE LAW

The Fair Debt Collection Practices Act covers collection of any debt incurred for personal, family, or household purposes. The act applies to:

1. Any person in the business of collecting debts owed to others;
2. Any creditor who, collecting from his or her own customers, uses a name other than his or her own.
3. Anyone who regularly collects or attempts to collect debts for another.

But not all debt collectors are subject to the act. It does not apply to banks, other lenders, or businesses that collect their own accounts using their own names. Nor does it cover them when they collect an isolated debt for another.

LOCATING A CUSTOMER

A covered debt collector may contact a person other than the customer only to discover or verify the customer's location. In doing so, the collector must:

1. Identify himself, but he can identify his employer only if expressly requested to do so;
2. Not reveal the consumer's indebtedness;

3. Not use a postcard or in any way reveal his debt collection activity;
4. Not communicate with that person more than once unless reasonably necessary.

If the collector learns the identity of an attorney who is representing the customer, the contact must be with that attorney.

CONTACTING THE CUSTOMER

The law allows a collector to make reasonable efforts to communicate with a customer about his or her debt. A covered collector may not contact a customer about his obligation:

1. At an inconvenient or unusual time (the hours between 8 a.m. and 9 p.m. are considered to be convenient);
2. At an inconvenient place;
3. At his or her place of employment if it is known the employer prohibits such contact;
4. If an attorney is known to represent the customer (the attorney should be contacted instead).

Contact also may not be made after the customer notifies the collector in writing that he or she refuses to pay a debt or objects to the contacts, but contact may be made to explain the possible consequences to the customer.

PROHIBITED TACTICS

The law prohibits harassing, oppressing, or abusive conduct in connection with collection of a debt. This includes but is not limited to:

1. The use or threat of violence or harm to the person, his or her reputation, or property;
2. Use of obscene language;
3. Publicizing the debt;
4. Annoying or repetitive telephone calls;
5. Anonymous phone calls;
6. False, deceptive, or misleading representations as to the collector's identity;
7. False representations of the status of the debt and the consequences of nonpayment;

Fair Debt Collection Practices Act

8. Failure to adequately disclose the reason for contacting the consumer;
9. Collecting an additional fee not authorized by law or the terms of the debt agreement;
10. Accepting a check postdated by more than five days except under specified written conditions;
11. Tricking a customer into accepting a collect call or telegram by concealing the true purpose of the call or telegram;
12. Communicating by postcard.

VALIDATING THE DEBT

Within five days after contacting a customer about paying his debt, the collector must send him a written notice informing him:

1. Of the amount of the debt;
2. Of the name of the creditor;
3. That the debt will be assumed to be valid unless disputed within thirty days;
4. That if disputed, the collector will verify it and send a copy of the verification or of a judgment against the consumer;
5. That on request the name and address of the original creditor (if changed) will be provided.

During a period when a debt is being verified, the collector may not attempt to obtain payment.

LEGAL REMEDIES

Any debt collector who intentionally fails to comply with this law may be sued for actual damages; additional damages as allowed by a court up to $1,000 (or the lesser of $500,000 or one percent of net worth in a class action suit); and court costs and reasonable attorneys' fees.

This explanation is not intended to be a complete or official summary of the Fair Debt Collection Practices Act.

APPENDIX G
STATE COLLECTION AGENCY LICENSING AUTHORITIES

ALASKA: Karl Luck, Director; Jennifer Strickler, Administrative Officer, Department of Commerce & Economic Development, Division of Occupational Licensing, Collection Agencies, Box 110806, Juneau, AK 99811-0806, (907) 465-2536

ARIZONA: Harold C. Feeney, Acting Superintendent, State Banking Department, 3225 N. Central, Suite 800, Phoenix, AZ 85012, (602) 255-4421, FAX (602) 255-4421

ARKANSAS: Rhonda K. Slayden, Director, State Board of Collection Agencies, 217 West Second Street, Suite 325, Little Rock, AR 72201, (501) 376-9814

COLORADO: Laura E. Udis, Executive Director, Collection Agency Board, 1525 Sherman St., Denver, CO 80203, (303) 866-5304 or (303) 620-4601

CONNECTICUT: Robert Focht, Director, Consumer Credit Division, Department of Banking, 44 Capitol Ave., Hartford, CT 06106, (203) 566-4560, Ext. 8119

FLORIDA: Linda Dilworth, Assistant Director, Division of Finance, Department of Banking and Finance, Capitol Bldg., Tallahassee, FL 32399-0350, (904) 488-4348

HAWAII: Verna Tomita, Executive Secretary, Professional and Vocational Licensing Division, Department of Commerce and Consumer Affairs, Box 3469, Honolulu, HI 96801, (808) 586-2694

IDAHO: Belton J. Patty, Director of Finance; Gavin Gee, Chief, Financial Institutions Bureau, Finance Examinations Bureau, Department of Finance, Statehouse Mall, Boise, ID 83720, (208) 334-2945

ILLINOIS: Saundra Vesey-Malwick, Board Liaison, Professional Services Section, Department of Professional Regulation, 320 W. Washington St., 3rd Floor, Springfield, IL 62786, (217) 785-0800

INDIANA: Lorraine Bigsbee, Deputy Commissioner of Collection Agencies, Office of the Secretary of State, 302 W. Washington St., Room E 111, Indianapolis, IN 46204, (317) 232-0093

IOWA: Attorney General, Consumer Protection Division, 1300 East Walnut, Hoover Building, Des Moines, IA 50319, (515) 281-5926

LOUISIANA: Larry Murray, Commissioner, Office of Financial Institutions, P.O. Box 94095, Baton Rouge, LA 70804-9095, (504) 925-4660

MAINE: Harry Giddinge, Deputy Superintendent, Bureau of Consumer Credit Protection, State House Station 35, Augusta, ME 04333, (207) 582-8718

MARYLAND: Allen T. Fell, Chairperson, Maryland Collection Agency Licensing Board, Commission of Consumer Credit, 501 St. Paul Pl., Baltimore, MD 21202, (301) 333-6330

MASSACHUSETTS: Cyra Narva, Supervisor of Loan Agencies, 100 Cambridge St., Boston, MA 02202, (617) 727-3141

MICHIGAN: Suzanne Jolicoeur, Licensing Administrator, Collection Practices Board, Box 30018, Lansing, MI 48909, (517) 373-1654, FAX (517) 373-2795

MINNESOTA: Dennis Pappenhagen, Director of Licensing, Department of Commerce, 133 E. 7th St., Saint Paul, MN 55101, (612) 296-6319, FAX (612) 296-4328

NEBRASKA: Allen J. Beermann, Administrator, Collection Agency Licensing Board, Secretary of State, 2300 State Capitol Bldg., Lincoln, NE 63509, (402) 471-2008

NEVADA: L. Scott Walshaw, Commissioner of Financial Institutions Division, Department of Commerce, 406 E. 2nd St., Carson City, NV 89710, (702) 687-4259, FAX (702) 687-6909

NEW JERSEY: James Fruschine, Acting Chief of Filing Services, Division of Commercial Recording, Department of State, CN308, Trenton, NJ 08625, (609) 530-6422

NEW MEXICO: Robert I. LaGrange, Director, Financial Institutions Division, 725 St. Michael Dr., Box 25101, Santa Fe, NM 87504, (505) 827-7100, FAX (505) 827-7107

NEW YORK: (Buffalo) Michael Mulderig, Division of Licensing, Room 113, City Hall, Buffalo, NY 14202, (716) 851-4951
(New York City) Richard Schrader, Acting Commissioner, Department of Consumer Affairs, 42 Broadway, New York, NY 10004, (212) 487-4444 or (212) 487-3956 or (212) 487-4051

NORTH CAROLINA: Frederick H. Mohn, Deputy Commissioner, Special Services Division, North Carolina Department of Insurance, Box 26387, Raleigh, NC 27611, (919) 733-2200

NORTH DAKOTA: Gary Preszler, Commissioner, Department of Banking & Financial Institutions, State Capitol, 13th Floor, 600 E. Boulevard Ave., Bismarck, ND 58505-0080, (701) 224-2253

OREGON: Sharlyn Rayment, Supervising Examiner, Collection Agency Program, Finance Section, 21 Labor and Industries Bldg., Salem, OR 97310, (503) 378-4140

Licensing Authorities 201

PUERTO RICO: Bureau of Enforcement, Department of Consumer Affairs, Commonwealth of Puerto Rico, Box 41059 Minillas Sta., Santurce, PR 00940

TENNESSEE: Betty Hughey, Administrator, Tennessee Collection Services Board, Volunteer Plaza, 500 James Robertson Pkwy., Nashville, TN 37219, (615) 741-1741

TEXAS: Guy Joyner, Esq., Legal Support Unit, Secretary of State, Statutory Documents Division, 221 E. 11th Street, Room 404, Austin, TX 78701, (512) 463-5559

UTAH: Peter VanAlstyne, Director, Department of Commerce, Division of Corporations and Commercial Code, Box 45801, Salt Lake City, UT 84145-0801, (801) 530-6026

VIRGIN ISLANDS: Clement Magras, Commissioner, Department of Licensing & Consumer Affairs, Golden Rock Shopping Center, Christiansted, St. Croix, VI 00820

WASHINGTON: Simon Tee, Program Manager, Department of Licensing Services, P.O. Box 9649, Olympia, WA 98507, (206) 586-4567

WEST VIRGINIA: Department of Taxation, Compliance Division, Box 229, Charleston, WV 25325, (304) 558-3333

WISCONSIN: Howard Quimby, Administrator, Division of Consumer Credit, Office of Commissioner of Banking, Box 7876, Madison, WI 53707, (608) 266-0898

WYOMING: Vickie Spires, Wyoming Collection Agency License Board, 2301 Central Ave., Barrett Bldg., 3rd Floor, Cheyenne, WY 82002, (307) 777-6313, FAX (307) 777-6005

INDEX

Affidavit of Identification, 137
Agencies, collection
  advance suit fees, 152–54
  balance confirmation, 152, 153
  cost, 148, 152–54
  coverage, 149
  Fair Debt Collection Practices Act, 146
  guidelines, 154
  insurance, 147
  licensing, 147, 199–201
  methods used, 149
  progress reports, 149
  selection, 146–50
  unethical, 150–52
  when to use, 145–46
  withdrawal of accounts, 150
Applications, credit
  commercial, 21–23
  confidentiality, 27
  consumer, 19–21
  Equal Credit Opportunity Act, 20–21, 175–81
  Fair Credit Reporting Act, 21, 183–85
  form, 16–18
  laws governing, 20–21, 175–81, 183–85
  notice, 180
  purpose, 15
  updating, 23
  veracity clause, 15
  verifying, 23–24
Arbitration, 167–69
Assets
  attaching, 137–40
  current, 39
  fixed, 39

Attorneys, collection
  agreement with, 157–58
  conduct of, 160
  cost, 158, 159
  dissatisfaction with, 159–60
  letters by, 158
  progress reports, 158
  role of, 158–59
  selection, 157–58

Balance ranges, 28–29
Balance sheets. *See* Financial statements.
Bank credit information
  balance ranges, 28–29
  information forms, 30–31
  rules, 29–32
  terminology, 28
Bank wire transfer, 114
Billing. *See* Fair Credit Billing Act.

Checks
  bounced, 30–32
  clearing, 30–32
  presenting as collection item, 32,33
Civic associations, 32–34
Commercial credit, definition of, 21
Communication, 57, 61–62
Company resources. *See* Resources, company.
Complaints, customer, 69–70, 108–9
Computers, 5
Confidentiality, 25, 27–28

Consumer credit, definition of, 19
Corporation, definition of, 22
Credit
   applications. See Applications, credit.
   associations, 32–34
   denial. See denial of credit.
   philosophy, 4
   reasons to extend, 3–4
   telephone inquiries, 24
Credit-granting strategy. See also Decision making.
   effectiveness of, 6–7
   factors affecting, 3
   selection of, 13–14
   support for, 14
Credit-reporting services
   cost, 36
   reliability, 38
   sample credit report, 37

Days' Sales Outstanding formula, 6–7
Decision making
   delegation authority, 46–47
   information needed for, 47–48
   objectives, 46
Defamatory statements 25, 27–28
Delinquency. See also Agencies, collection; Attorneys, collection; Letters, collection; Mediation; Settlements; Small claims court; Telephone collection.
   follow-up, 65
   reasons for, 61–63
   reminder letters, 67–69
   response to initial inquiry, 69–70
Denial of credit
   generally, 183–84
   alternatives to, 49–50
   laws governing, 20–21, 48, 175–81, 183–85
   notification, 48, 180
   reason for, 21, 180
   source identification, 48–49
Discrimination. See Equal Credit Opportunity Act.
Disputes, 26–27

Dollar Days Outstanding formula, 7, 8–11

Equal Credit Opportunity Act, 20–21, 48, 175–81
Equipment, 5
Execution of judgment, 136–40

Fair Credit Billing Act, 27, 187–90
Fair Credit Reporting Act, 21, 183–85
Fair Debt Collection Practices Act, 146, 195–97
Faxing, 117
Financial statements. See also Ratios.
   analysis of, 39–44
Follow-up, collection
   after telephone collection, 116–17
   cost of, 76–77
   systems, 66
   timing, 66–67
Formulas
   Days' Sales Outstanding, 6–7
   Dollar Days Outstanding, 7, 8–11

Garnishment exemption notice, 140–42
Good faith payment, 111–12
Grace period, 65

Harassment. See Fair Debt Collection Practices Act.
History, credit, 21, 179–80

Inflation, 75–76
Interest rates, 71–75
Interviewing techniques, 35–36
Investigation, credit, 47–48

Legal action. See Attorneys, collection; Small claims court.
Letters, collection
   benefits of, 79
   closer line, 85–86
   elements of, 82–87
   K.I.S.S. principle, 79–80
   laws governing, 99
   readability index, 173–74

recognition line, 83
rules for writing, 79–82
sample "Before" & "After," 88–97
signature line, 85–86
Liabilities
  current, 39–40
  long-term, 40
Limits, credit
  established customers, 52–53
  new customers, 51–52
  seasonal customers, 54

Mediation
  collecting, 166–67
  definition, 163
  finding mediator, 167
  phases, 164–66
  when to use, 164
Motivation, 56

NACM ADR Program, 168–169
Nonpayment. *See* Delinquency.

Partnership, 22
Payment agreement, 111–16
Personnel
  generally, 5–6
  credit information from, 55–56
  delegating authority, 46–47
Profit margins, 71

Rating, credit, 188–89
Ratios
  accounts receivable turnover, 40, 43–44
  aftertax corporate profit to corporate domestic income, 71, 72–73
  current, 40, 42
  current debt to net worth, 40, 42
  inventory turnover, 40, 43
  quick, 40, 42
Receivables, age of, 6–7
References, checking, 23–24. *See also* Bank credit information; Credit-reporting services; Letters, collection; Telephone collection.
Rejections, credit. *See* Denial of credit.
Reminder letters, 67–69
Report, credit. *See* Credit-reporting services; Fair Credit Reporting Act.
Request for Order for Disclosure, 139
Resources, company, 5–6

Sales philosophy, 4
Satisfaction of judgment, 134–35
Settlements
  deciding, 125
  structure of offer, 124
  timing, 124
  when to settle, 123, 124
Skiptracing, 129, 191–94
Small claims court
  claim limit, 127
  collecting judgment, 134
  counterclaims, 130–33
  court appearance, 133
  deciding, 128–29, 140–43
  execution of judgment, 136–40
  filing fee, 129–30
  filing requirements, 127
  filing suit, 129–30
  garnishment exemption notice, 140–42
  notification of decision, 123–24
  notification of parties, 130
  sample claim form, 131–32
  satisfaction of judgment, 134–35
  writ of execution, 136, 138
Sole proprietorship, 21–22
Source identification, 48–49
Strategy. *See* Credit-granting strategy.

Telephone collection
  agreements, 111–16
  fact-finding, 106–11
  faxing, 117
  good faith payment, 111–12
  identification, 105–6
  preparation, 102–5
  when to use, 101–2

Trade associations, 32–34
Trade credit information
  exchange of, 27
  request for, 25
  right to, 24
  rights of inquiry, 25–27
  verification, 23–24
Training, 56–57

Wolner's rules, 2, 22, 30, 45, 57, 59–60, 77, 79–80, 107, 116, 150